An Introduction to Communication

The Fundamentals

HIMANI CHAUDHRY

NOTION PRESS

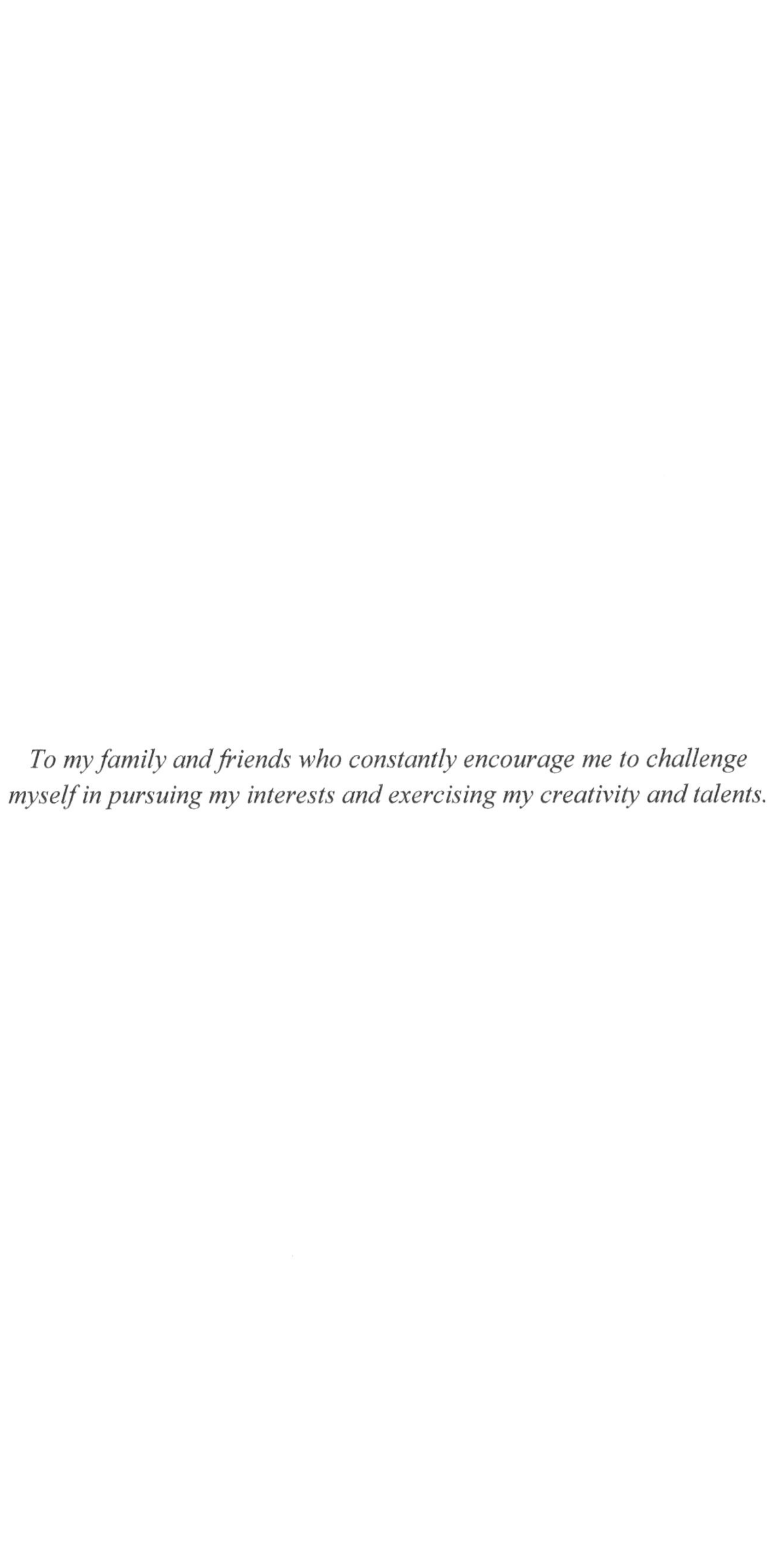

To my family and friends who constantly encourage me to challenge myself in pursuing my interests and exercising my creativity and talents.

Contents

Figures

Acknowledgments

To begin with, I express deep gratitude to my parents due to whose blessing my world advances, and it is with their blessings that I take this step forward, like all others I have, thus far.

I must express my appreciation and sincere thanks for the constant encouragement, support, advice and forbearance of my husband Mr. Venkiteswaran M., especially during the writing of this book.

Whilst I take personal responsibility for this work, I wish to acknowledge a host of sources that inspired me to come up with this book. These sources have been duly acknowledged and mentioned at appropriate places.

Further, I would also like to express my sincere thanks to my colleague Ms. Surumi Salim, for her constant encouragement and support.

I must also thank those well-wishers who kindly advised me regarding my manuscript, but prefer to remain unnamed.

Any suggestion for the development of the book shall be solicited and thankfully acknowledged.

Thanks are due of course, to the Divine, that makes it all possible!

1. Communication

"The imparting or exchanging of information by speaking, writing, or using some other medium is termed as 'Communication'. It is the successful conveying or sharing of ideas and feelings."

— Oxford English Dictionary

Communication is the act of transferring information from one person, group or organization to another. The term 'Communication' is said to have descended etymologically from the Latin noun 'communicatio', meaning 'a sharing or imparting'. It derives its meaning from the Latin verb 'communicare' which means 'to make common', 'to exchange' or 'share'.

Communication can be defined as sharing, transfer or transmission of information or understanding from one person or group to another. It is the giving, receiving or exchanging of ideas, messages, information, or signals through appropriate media, enabling individuals or groups to seek or give information, or to express emotions and facilitate (better) understanding. It is a dynamic, goal-oriented approach of satisfying the human urge to communicate and developing mutual understanding which is the basis of all human relationships. Communication is said to be a social intercourse involving the process of transmitting messages and exchanging emotions, facts, ideas, opinions, values etc., from one person, group or place to another through body-language and skills such as speaking and writing. It ranges from simple facial expressions or gestures to the most advanced technologies. Receiving, understanding and interpretation are integral to communication.

Definitions of Communication

'Communication' is an intercourse through symbols, words, messages etc., and is a means through which members of an organization share meaning and understanding with one another. It has been defined in different terms by different scholars. The following are some of the important definitions of communication:

According to *Katz and Kahn*, "communication is the exchange of information and the transmission of meaning. It is the very essence of a social system of an organization".

J. Pearson and *P. Nelson* define 'communication' as "the process of understanding and sharing meaning".

In communication, sharing occurs when one conveys thoughts, feelings, ideas or insights to oneself or to others.

According to *Allen Louis*, "communication is the sum of all the things one person does; when he wants to create understanding in the mind of another. It involves a systematic and continuous process of telling, listening and understanding."

Communication is defined as "the transmission and interchange of facts, ideas, feelings or course of action", by *Leland Brown*,

Communication "is an exchange of facts, ideas, opinions or emotions by two or more persons" according to Newman and Summer.

McFarland has defined communication as, "a process of meaningful interaction among human beings. More specifically, it is the process by which meanings are perceived and understandings are reached among human beings."

According to *Keith Davis* "communication is a process of passing information and understanding from one another".

Peter Little: Communication is a process by which information is transmitted between individuals and/or organizations so that an understanding response results.

John Adair says "Communication is essentially the ability of one person to make contact with another and make himself or herself understood."

According to *Murphy, Hildebrandt, Thomas*, "Communication is a process of transmitting and receiving verbal and non-verbal messages. It is considered effective when it achieves the desired response or reaction from the receiver."

William Newman and *Charles Summer*: Communication is an exchange of ideas, facts, opinions or emotions of two or more persons.

In communication, sharing occurs when one conveys thoughts, feelings, ideas or insights to oneself or to others.

Need for Communication

Estimates say that people spend more time communicating than on any other complex activity in life. Human communication takes place at all levels, every day in nearly every environment, whether it is the simplest intrapersonal buck-up, a slight nod of head in agreement or disagreement, a presentation in a board room or a news telecast on the television.

The need for communication arises from the need for survival. Every instance of communication is motivated by basic needs of connectivity and information exchange. However, human needs in terms of communication go beyond the instinctive needs like hunting, mating, preying etc., exhibited by other creatures. Human communication is more complex than these and has varied manifestations ranging from simple gestures to the most advanced communication technologies. Also, it has several objectives to it. Humans seek to communicate in order to influence people, bring about changes in attitudes, motivate others and establish and maintain relationships with them. Communication among humans involves the use of language, which is a store-house of previously accepted complex codes agreed upon by the communicating parties.

Objectives of Communication

The purpose of communication is as varied as human emotion. One of the most basic purposes of communication is transferring information in order to produce greater understanding. However, there are several reasons and purposes for which people communicate. It could be to enquire, inform, remind, express, argue, discuss, etc. Humans communicate to:

1. Express feelings and emotions: Humans constantly experience the need to express feelings about people, places, objects, events, policies, and ideas and opinions and emotions such as joy, sorrow, anger, fear, satisfaction, disappointment etc. These may be expressed with the use of appropriate gestures, facial expressions or in words. This form of communication is called 'Affective communication'.

2. Convey information: People share knowledge, information, significant details, main points and facts about various aspects of the world in which they live and technologies they use. This form of communication is called 'Informative communication'. Informative messages attempt to present a truthful and unbiased view of everything.

3. Persuade or influence: Most people need to, and thus attempt to influence the beliefs or actions of others through their communication with them. This is referred to as 'Persuasive communication'. This form of communication plays a key role in a number of professions. Salespersons, lawyers, politicians, public relations departments frequently employ persuasive communication in their professions. Advertising is the most prominent form of persuasive communication in the contemporary world.

4. Facilitate social interaction: Society has strong expectations about how others should conduct themselves in various social situations. Social norms such as those of greeting and leave-taking, telephone and table etiquette are some expected social behaviours. All these social interactions and most others are an integral part of personal

and social communication. 'Ritualistic communication' is the process through which people meet all social expectations and carry out social interactions and communication.

5. Express creativity: Creative expression is a human need that prompts 'Imaginative communication'. While day dreams may be a creative expression limited to oneself, inventing and sharing fiction, jokes, poetry, plays and so on, are all ways for humans to communicate thoughts, ideas and imagination to others.

Importance of Communication

Humans communicate at various levels – from the simplest of interpersonal and small-group exchanges among friends and family to mass-communication as experienced in public speeches, magazines, or news broadcasts and so on. Communication has been greatly instrumental in shaping human life in all its spheres–including family, education, employment, business, research, technology, religion, culture and politics etc.

Thus, communication is used at all times, in every environment, including in the workplace. Communication is a vital tool that helps people in co-existing peacefully and also in sharing ideas, and network building, delegating responsibilities and managing workplace affairs. Good communication is vital to a healthy, efficient work environment. It helps people to understand (process) information more accurately and quickly. Almost all transactions in the world of business result from communication. Excellence in communication enables people to achieve their goals and succeed in their careers.

Communication has played a significant part in making the world as it is today, and continues to shrink the world through more and more robust methods and models of communication.

The importance of communication can be illustrated thus:

1. Communication eases the processes of planning, organising and co-ordination in any given environment.
2. Communication is the key to establishing and maintaining cordial relationships in personal as well as professional life, since it bridges the gaps that are likely to occur in mutual understanding, in the absence of (effective) communication.
3. It is a key aid in decision-making as it enables a person or organisation to make informed decisions.
4. It facilitates timely and correct action.
5. Efficient communication boosts the morale and keeps people motivated.
6. Effective communication eliminates the scope for misunderstandings in and thus assists in effective leadership.
7. Communication plays an important role in problem-solving and conflict management.
8. It enables people to manage interactions at personal level and also within businesses and organisations.
9. Since good communication facilitates exchange of ideas, opinions, decisions and advices, it instils the right attitude and behaviour in people.

Modes of Communication

'Mode' is a term that describes the way something is expressed or done. Thus, the term 'Mode of Communication' describes the way or the manner in which communication is carried out. Communication is not just putting words onto paper anymore. It can be carried out in several ways, depending on the nature and context of the information, purpose of communication and the motivation, abilities and communication needs of the sender (and receiver). At every occasion one has to make a choice regarding the mode of communication he/she uses, in order to communicate in the most suitable way. For instance, written communication is used for purposes such as, sending emails, applications and notices etc., while oral communication is combined with visual communication for meetings and presentations. Further, knowledge of the skills necessary to effectively use a specific communication mode also determines a person's use of it. Thus, information can be shared using various (combinations of) modes of communication. It may be noted that the medium or channel through which communication or information is conveyed is different from the mode using which communicative intent is expressed.

Differences in the selection of modes of communication by people arise from differences in their abilities, thinking, perception, preferred style of communication and perspectives, apart from the differences in their language proficiency and intelligibility.

Typically, modes of communication include speaking, facial expressions, gestures and writing. However, these may also include the use of graphic symbols, visuals etc, such as emoticons and 'gifs' in informal communication of today.

Communication usually draws on multiple modes for communication, such as linguistical, gestural, visual and aural, and so, is referred to as multimodal communication.

Classification of Modes of Communication

The main modes of communication may be classified under 'Verbal' and 'Non-verbal'.

Verbal Modes of Communication

Verbal communication refers to any communication that makes use of words to communicate with others, in contrast to using gestures or mannerisms. These words can be written and spoken, both. Therefore, 'Verbal' communication comprises both, spoken and written communication, though many a time in general terms it is used to refer to only spoken communication. The verbal mode of communication is about the words that a sender/speaker chooses, and how they are perceived and interpreted by the receiver/listener.

Linguistical or Alphabetic Communication

Linguistical or Alphabetic mode of communication mainly refers to *written* or *spoken* (*Verbal*) communication that relies on words to create meaning. It conveys messages by means of print/text and speech/audio. The linguistical mode includes word choice, organising words into meaningful, coherent units (phrases, sentences, paragraphs etc.), and developing cohesive ideas. It is one of the most popular and frequently used modes of communication, since words, whether spoken or written, add depth and emotion to communication. It is often used with other modes such as images or visuals, to make communication more substantial.

Written Communication

Written communication is a type of verbal communication. It refers to the communication carried out using the written word. The choice of words in written communication is of utmost importance since this mode of communication relies only on their interpretation. Letters, emails, notices and any such messages that are sent through written word/text is a form of written communication. Written communication is sometimes also referred to as 'Linguistical' mode.

Oral Communication

The communication through the spoken word is called 'oral' mode of communication. It is also called 'spoken' or 'vocal' communication sometimes. It can be carried out through electronic media such as voice mail, radio, telephonic communication, etc., or as face-to-face interaction including informal conversations, staff/official meetings, public speeches etc.

Aural Communication

This mode uses the 'audio' mode (hearing/listening) for communication through speech sounds, be it through sounds or spoken audios such as in an audio book. It includes not only the sounds of spoken words but also the use of tone of voice, accent, emphasis, pitch, and other speech features in spoken language, apart from music, volume, rhythm. Sound catches people's attention, and so the use of the aural mode to transmit messages is frequent.

Non-verbal Modes of Communication

Nonverbal communication is usually understood as communication through the modes of communicating other than words (non-linguistic). It is often therefore, said to be communication beyond language cues (verbal cues) through actions and attributes of humans, especially those of shared social (or cultural) significance, that stimulate meaning in other humans. It is the sending and receiving of messages using all aspects of communication other than the words, that is 'visual cues', as against 'verbal cues'. Such messages can be conveyed through gesture; facial expression; posture or body language; eye contact; personal appearance; objects such as clothing and adornment; symbols and infographics; use of space, distance and time; etc. Nonverbal communication can occur through any sensory channel - sight, sound, smell, touch or taste.

Gestural Communication

Gestural Communication typically represents the use of physical movements and body language to communicate messages and the way any such movement is interpreted to communicate meaning. Facial expressions, hand signals and gestures and body language are all interaction between people using the gestural mode. Gestural communication is vital especially, to face-to-face communication.

This mode of communication, combined with aural, visual, linguistic and even spatial modes, makes communication better and more understandable. However, it can also be used individually, (such as in Sign

Language) given that both the communicating parties (sender and receiver) have their own common points of reference and meanings to have an understandable and meaningful communication.

Visual Communication

Visual Communication can be termed as one of the oldest modes of communication when symbols, etchings and drawings were used for the purpose of conveying meaning. It relies on visual information to communicate meaning. A visual has the potential to convey an idea more quickly and as effectively as most other modes of communication. This is because images can better engage the senses and thus convey information more easily than merely with words. Combined with other modes such as the linguistical mode, it can make communication very quick, easy and effective. The use of images, charts, graphs, maps etc. in official communication are examples of the visual mode.

Spatial Communication

Spatial Communication refers to the use of physical space to convey certain meanings and messages. It involves the arrangement or the organization of elements and items in physical space, and elaborates upon the physical closeness between people and objects. For example, the physical layout of an office space can communicate the organisational structure and approach followed by that office. Proxemics too comes into interplay in spatial communication.

Although interpersonal communication can encompass oral, written, and non-verbal forms of communication, the term is usually applied to spoken communication that takes place between two or more individuals on a personal or face to face level.

Multimodal Communication

Multimodal Communication can be referred to as the communication mechanics that involves varied modes such as language, gestures, symbols etc., for communication. It is a holistic way of communication since it makes use of several modes of communication. Five different modes are frequently used to accentuate communication under multimodal communication.

These 5 modes are:

1. Linguistical or Alphabetic: Using either written or spoken words.
2. Gestural: Using gestures, movement, and expression etc.
3. Visual: Using images, videos, and graphics.
4. Aural: Using sounds, music, pitch, tone, rhythm, etc.
5. Spatial: Using proximity, physical coordination, positions.

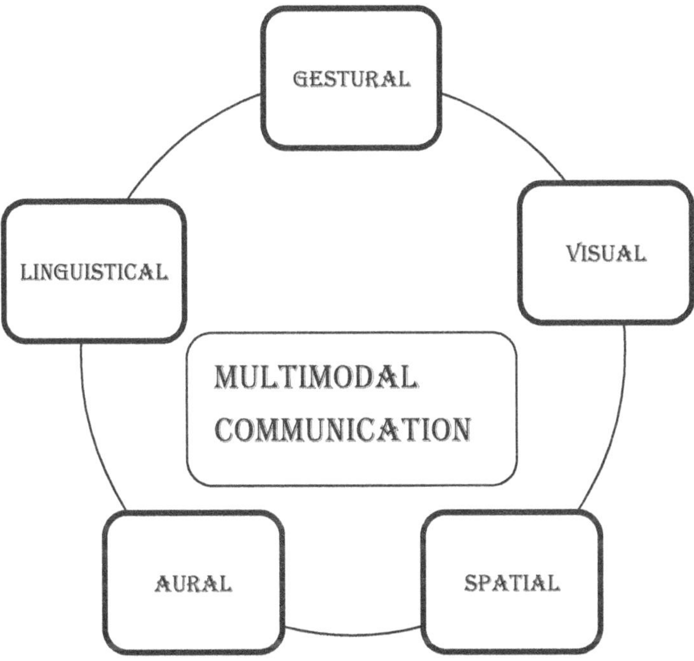

Fig 1: Multimodal Communication

Main Elements of Communication

Clearly worded, unambiguous messages that maintain an appropriate tone translate as effective communication. Effective communication is an outcome of the role played by certain key elements that constitute the entire process of communication. The essential elements or steps constituting the process of communication are:

Source or Sender

The foundation of a communication process is layered by the 'sender' who is the 'source' of a message. A sender initiates communication by composing, encoding and sending a message. He/she composes it depending upon the situation, the nature and the importance of the information to be sent.

Message

A message may be a thought, an idea, a gesture, a symbol, a picture, a report or even a blink, wink or smile. A message can be verbal or non-verbal, vocal or written.

Channel

The medium or mode used by the sender to communicate the message is referred as the channel of communication. A channel links the sender and the receiver. Computers, telephones, chatbots, radio and television are some examples of channels for communication.

Proper selection of the channel is of prime importance for effective communication.

Receiver

A receiver is one of the most vital components in the process of communication, along with a sender and a message. Upon receiving a message, he/she decodes it, understands it and perceives the communicated idea.

Feedback

The response of a receiver to the message from the sender is referred to as 'feedback'. Receiving feedback is an indication for the sender that the message has been correctly interpreted. It is the final step in the communication process. Through 'Feedback' the sender is assured that the message has been effectively encoded, sent, decoded and comprehended. An analysis of the feedback helps the sender improve future messages. Feedback, like the (original) message, can be verbal or non-verbal and is transmitted through a carefully chosen channel, replicating the process of sending in communication. Feedback can be positive or constructive and negative or neutral.

Environment

The common context and shared understanding form the backdrop of communication between communicating parties. This is what is referred to as 'environment' in the process of communication.

Noise

The internal as well as external forces which disrupt the smooth flow of communication anywhere in the entire cycle of communication are known as 'noise' or 'barriers of communication'. Noise can get induced and interfere with accurate reception and decoding of a message even though a speaker may have sent a clear message. Noise can be technical, semantic or environmental, depending on the type and mode of communication. The inability of radio antennae in decoding a different radio signal, (FM to AM radio or vice versa, for example) is noise of '**technical**' nature. Inability or difficulty faced by a sender or a receiver in encoding or decoding a message because they do not understand the other's language or symbols interferes with their communication and this is an instance of '**semantic**' noise. And so is the ambiguity induced in a message due to unfamiliar or multiple meanings of words or sentences. Any distractions or physical noise encountered during communication is termed as '**environmental**' noise. It can refer to any background sounds that interfere with the encoding, transmission or decoding of the message.

Encoding and Decoding

Encoding or encrypting is the process of arranging the message into a series of symbols, words or pictures, such that its true intent can be interpreted by the intended receiver. Encoding is an important step in the communication process as inappropriate encoding can cause the process to fail.

Decoding or decrypting refers to the process of converting the received message into intelligible form and interpreting it. This is an important step in the receiver's interpretation and comprehending of the message. Wrong decoding of a message can cause a receiver to misconstrue the message, thus defeating the true intent of the communication.

Essentials of Communication

The ability to communicate effectively is necessary to carry out the thoughts and visions of an organization to the people. The essentials of effective communication are:

i. A common communication environment;

ii. Co-operation and understanding between the sender and the receiver;

iii. Selection of appropriate channel;

iv. Correct encoding and decoding of the message;

v. Receipt of desired response and feedback;

vi. Means to override noise.

The Process of Communication

The process of communication refers to the transmission of information (a *message*) from a *sender* to a *receiver* through a selected medium or *channel*, overcoming all barriers that affect its transmission. The process requires the sender and the receiver to interact within a common context conforming to shared cultural, social, religious and national norms and ethics, by means of a message and a medium. Apart from the shared frame of reference comprised of common understanding of norms and ethics, it is necessary that the sender and receiver co-operate with each other.

Communication is a cyclic process of dynamic interaction that begins with the sender's sending of a message and ends with sender's receiving a response (*feedback*) to his message. Figure 1 depicts the basic model of the process of communication.

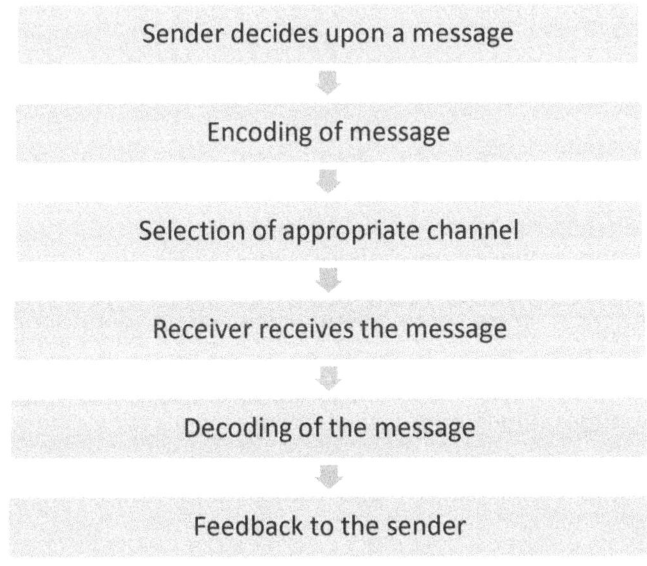

Fig 2. Basic Model of the Process of Communication

Principles of Effective Communication

A principle may be defined as *a fundamental statement or a proposition that serves as the foundation for a system, through the application of which predetermined objectives can be achieved.* The principles of communication enable individuals to generate information in a manner that is best suited for the operation of communication to be smooth and successful. They are vital in enriching the communication processes and making communication precise and meaningful. Further, an understanding of principles of communication is necessary for members of an organisation to promote effective communication. These principles also enable individuals to understand the different purposes of communication that are instructing, informing, convincing, conveying, persuading, requesting, warning, reassuring, asking, and stating.

Effective communication is fundamental to success in all areas of human life. While effective communication paves the way to the growth and success of an individual as well as an organisation, a lack of appropriate communication can handicap their smooth functioning and professional growth. So, to have error-free, effective communication, it must be ensured that the message is accurate and unambiguous, specifies the communication objective, and utilizes the most appropriate communication technique/medium in order for the receiver to interpret the message according to the sender's expectation.

To transmit effective oral or written messages, certain principles must be followed. There are seven core principles of communication, also called '*The 7 C's of Effective Communication*' that are considered best practice in both written and oral communication. These principles provide guidelines for the choice of content and style of communication of a message. University of Wisconsin professor Scott M. Cutlip and Allen H. Center first introduced the '*Seven Cs of Communication*' in 1952 in their textbook in the field of public relations 'Effective Public Relations'. These principles are outlined below:

The 7 C's of Communication

- Completeness
- Conciseness
- Consideration
- Concreteness
- Courtesy
- Clearness
- Correctness

Ahead, we discuss these principles of effective communication.

1. **Completeness:** The communicator must ensure that the information being communicated is complete and adequate in all respect, that is to say, it must include all the relevant information required by the intended audience. Incomplete or inadequate messages cause miscommunication and even delays in the action to be taken whereas complete information answers all queries of the receiver and helps them in better decision-making. Further, the information must be consistent with the organizational objectives, plans, policies and procedures and also with the purpose of the communication at hand. Inconsistency in communication can harm corporate interests. The message should be complete, i.e. it must include all the relevant information as required by the intended audience.

2. **Conciseness:** A concise message is complete without being overly wordy or overly economising on words. It is precise and to the point. It should be brief and be able to state/convey whatever has to be communicated, in the fewest possible words without sacrificing the quality or purpose of the message. A short, brief message is more comprehensive and helps in retaining the receiver's attention. Avoiding unnecessary information is a right step in the direction.

3. **Consideration:** In order to make communication effective, the sender must relate to the target recipient, take into consideration

the receiver's viewpoint, knowledge level, mindset, background, etc., and create an appropriate message accordingly.

4. **Concreteness:** The message must be specific and definite rather than have vague and generalized statements. It should provide clearly worded concrete information/facts, so as to substantiate the rest of what is stated in the message.

5. **Courtesy:** The message must at all times be polite and courteous in its tone and wording. It should be focussed and appreciative of its recipient/audience and be positive and courteous in its approach. The message should not be biased and must evidently show respect for the recipient.

6. **Clearness:** Clarity in communication refers to the accurate transfer of ideas or information etc. from the sender's side to the receiver. There should be clarity in all aspects of the communication--the idea which is to be communicated and the purpose of communication. A clear understanding of the subject and the purpose bring about clarity in the message. The message must be framed in simple unambiguous words such that it interprets the same to the receiver, as the sender evokes a response from the receiver that meets the expectations of the sender. Complex or ambiguous messages can result in faulty communication or lack of it, giving rise to complexities. Messages, especially the long-distance ones, must therefore be distilled into simpler terms. It should also be ensured that both, the sender and the receiver are conversant with the language, inherent assumptions, and the mechanics of the communication and that no room for misinterpretation is left.

7. **Correctness:** The message being communicated must have accuracy in the facts, figures, and information being conveyed and the desired level of language with regard to both, expression as well as the correctness of grammar, punctuation, and spellings.

Some other principles attributed to effective communication are:

Continuity: All communication flowing between two communicating parties should stem from the initial communication made in that regard/context. That is, it should re-iterate or make reference to the previous communication on the same subject. This enables the sender to maintain continuity and avoid gaps in communication and the receiver to recall or refer the previous communication in the thread. Gaps in communication can lead to confusion.

Consistency: Communication is an unending process. It should be in accordance with the policies laid down for it by the organization. That is, the information conveyed must be consistent with the organizational objectives, policies, plans, procedures and processes. An inconsistent message can distort understanding and harm the communicator's purpose or interests.

Further, reinforcement of a message through clever repetition enables the receiver/audience to understand new concepts and ideas, learn new behaviour, and mentally rehearse how to respond to the content within the message. It also helps the sender to be more consistent.

Credibility: Credibility is an important criterion of effective communication. A message sent from a position of reliability and authority is received with high regard for the competency of the sender, by the receiver. This is because the trustworthiness of the sender that reflects in his/her actions generates belief in the earnestness of the sender. If the sender is trusted by the receiver, communication is effective.

Channel: Selecting and using an effective communication channel makes communication effective, since via an effective channel the message reaches its destination well in time, to the right person, and without distortion, filtering or omission. Further, the use of an established channel of communication ensures that the receiver receives the message through a channel he/she uses and respects. Creating new channels for communication can make communication difficult/obscure.

Competence: Communication must take into account the capability or competence of its audience. Communications are most effective when they require the least amount of effort in terms of understanding, on the part of the recipient.

Barriers to Communication

The word barrier means an obstacle, a hindrance or simply a problem. Problems and difficulties often arise in the path of transmission of a message, and they either completely or partially block the process of communication. All obstacles or interferences which affect not only the smooth transmission of information or a message, but also the understanding and/or acceptance of it are termed 'Barriers to Communication'. Communication Barriers result from inadequacies that tend to distort communication and make it less effective or unsuccessful.

No matter how efficient the communication system is, barriers do occur more often than not. These are caused due to varied factors such as system failure or fault in its design, and so on. The barriers that can occur in the process of communication are physical, sociological and psychological forces (whether external or internal) that impede the planning, organization, transmission or understanding of a message. They impede communication by either entirely preventing it, filtering out a part of it, or by giving it a different (often distorted or incorrect) meaning, depending on the stage of the communication process at which it manifests. All such barriers hinder the smooth functioning of an office/organisation or any other set up.

Based on the stage of manifestation, barriers to communication can be classified as:

Sender-oriented Barriers
These are lack of clarity about the purpose of communication, lack of planning, faulty encoding of the message due to improper choice of words, difference in perception, choice of wrong channel, etc.

Channel-oriented Barriers
These include noise, incorrect selection of medium or channel, technical shortcomings, etc.

Receiver-oriented Barriers

These barriers include improper decoding, lack of interest, poor listening skills, difference in perception and level of comprehension, attitudinal biases, communication load[1], etc.

Types of Barriers to Communication

Physical or Environmental Barriers

i) **Noise** – There is often a disruption in communication at the transmission level on account of Noise, it being one of the most common barriers in communication. Physical barriers are closely related to noise as they can obstruct the communication transmission process. The term Noise is often used to refer to not only unwanted sounds but also any persistent or random disturbance which reduces, obscures or confuses the clarity of a message. Noise encompasses all the hindrances or disturbances in communication that include poor signals or network, breakdown of communication media, faulty office equipment, etc., apart from actual noise in the environment due to external factors like noisy machines and equipment, traffic, loudspeakers, transport, crowds etc., that tend to cause obstruction in the process of communication. Noise can also be visual, audio-visual, written, physical or psychological in form.

ii) **Time** – Time becomes a barrier to communication when the communication has to take place over long geographic distances, especially across different time zones. Further, any communication process which is quite time-consuming can be a barrier to effective and timely communication.

iii) **Distance** – Physical distance between communicating parties too can hinder the communication process since it does not allow face-to-face communication. Inefficient or unsuitable space layout can be such a communication barrier, for instance, in an office.

---

[1]*The amount and complexity of messages received by the receiver are refered to as' communication load'.*

iv) **Choice of Medium** – Different media of communication are suitable for communicating for different purposes and at different times. So, before selecting one of the media for communication it is vital to consider the relative merits and limitations of each. In case the medium used for communication is not accurate, or appropriate, it becomes a barrier to effective communication. For instance, if a sender selects the medium with which the receiver is not familiar or not well acquainted, communication may be distorted or fail entirely.

v) **Climate** – Extreme weather conditions can lead to distraction and lack of focus and cause errors in communication on the part of the sender. Similarly, bad weather conditions may also obstruct the transmission or reception of communication. They can thus, be barriers to communication.

vi) **Technical Defects** – Technical and mechanical problems and defects in equipment and instruments of communication also create physical barriers in communication. For instance, a dysfunctional telephone line, a faulty computer, keyboard or fax machine can lead to non-transmission of messages.

Physiological or Biological Barriers

Disability – Physical defects or disabilities of the sender or receiver, such as speech defects like stammering, mumbling while speaking, hearing defects, weak vision, etc., too hinder smooth communication and so, are regarded as barriers to communication.

Language or Semantic Barriers

Barriers related to language or its meaning or interpretation (semantics) can cause obstructions in the process of communication either during the encoding or receiving, decoding or understanding of the message.

Difficulties in communication arise when the meaning intended by the sender is quite different from the meaning understood by the receiver or if the connotative meaning understood by the recipient doesn't align with the intended meaning of the message. Language or Semantic barriers can also arise due to:

i) **Use of jargon or unfamiliar terminology** – Use of technical jargon, register or terminology with which the receiver of the message is not familiar or comfortable, can cause either misinterpretation of meaning or failure in understanding it altogether, causing the communication to be unsuccessful.

ii) **Ambiguity** – Different connotative interpretation of words or phrases and ambiguity in the message can be barriers in communication. Ambiguity may arise due to different semantic features inherent in a language.

iii) **Absence of common language** – Differences in the language used by the communicating parties on account of regional differences etc., or absence of a common language amounts to the absence of a common medium of communication, and leads to inadequate interpretation/communication or failure of communication. These therefore, interpret as barriers since they can create problems in communication.

Psychological Barriers

Communication is an activity that aims to create understanding, Opinions, prejudices, attitudes, emotions, status consciousness, etc. deeply affect the ability of a person to communicate, since communication largely depends on the mental state or mindset of a person. All problems arising due to stress, perception or psychological issues therefore essentially affect the process of communication and are regarded as psychological barriers. Psychological barriers to communication are barriers that are created in the mind. Extreme work conditions, selective perception, poor retention, recaller span of attention, personal prejudices, complexes, or biases are some causes of hindrance in the smooth flow of communication. They thus amount to being barriers to communication.

Cross-cultural or Socio-cultural Barriers

People are more often than not, conditioned by their cultures and social values. They develop their habits pertaining to work, communication, etc. according to their cultural conditioning. Individuals of different social or cultural groups have different norms, values, etiquette, and behaviours. Differences arising from cultural diversity and differences in social status and values many a time cause differences in the interpretation of messages. They thus, often obstruct communication or even cause it to fail.

Cultural diversity within a country, and cultural differences between people from different countries, can be major barriers to communication. This is because, people of every culture develop certain specific habits of working, communicating, eating, dressing etc. according to their cultural conditioning. They can find it difficult to get through to people who come from a culture alien to them, and who have different habits.

Personal Barriers

Further, barriers to communication can be personal, based on the attitude and thinking of the sender and the receiver. These manifest as Interpersonal or Intrapersonal Barriers to Communication since they hinder or obstruct a free flow of communication.

Notes

----

2. Types of Communication

"Any act by which a person gives to or receives from the other, information about his needs, desires, perceptions, knowledge, or affective states. Communication may be intentional or unintentional, may involve conventional or unconventional signals, may take linguistic or non-linguistic forms, and may occur through spoken or other modes."

In general terms, communication can be classified as Verbal and Non-verbal. Communication carried out through words is called verbal communication whereas non-verbal communication includes body language, para-language (nonverbal cues like facial expressions, body stance, and tone of voice) and various types of visuals, signs and symbols. It can also be classified into oral and written communication. Listening and speaking being the two aspects of oral communication, while written communication manifests in various forms such as circulars, reports, notices, letters, e-mails, bulletins, telegrams, brochures etc., especially in the scenario of an official or formal set up.

However, there is more to this classification than these simple dichotomies (verbal and non-verbal; oral and written). The definitions, classification and perspectives on communication have evolved much over time, like all else. Communication can be classified into various types based on different parameters:

1. Based on Mode of Interaction or Expression

2. Based on Purpose and Style/ Number of Receivers

3. Based on Organisational Structure

4.   Based on Direction of Flow

Ahead, let us take a look at these classifications.

Based on Mode of Expression or Interaction

Humans use verbal and nonverbal cues to accomplish a number of personal and relational goals, the most important and dynamic being communication. Thus, based on the mode of interaction, communication can be classified into the following types:

1.   Verbal Communication
2.   Non-verbal Communication
3.   Visual Communication

Verbal Communication

Verbal Communication is an exchange of information by means of words, whether written or oral. It consists of speaking, listening, writing, reading etc. It is the most preferred mode of communication. Verbal communication can be one-to-one, or in group meeting (one-to-many), or over the phone. It manifests in the form of talks, public addresses, discussions, telephonic conversations, audio-visual media, speeches, meetings and conferences, lectures, social get-togethers, training sessions, etc.

Verbal Communication can be spontaneous as in the case of a face-to-face conversation or pre-prepared, when in the form of a discussion, speech etc. Verbal communication that takes place directly between people is known as face-to-face communication.

Verbal communication is of two types:

1. Oral Communication
2. Written Communication

Oral Communication

In Oral Communication information and understanding is transferred through spoken words. It is predominantly referred to as 'speech communication'. Oral communication can be had either through face-to-face conversations or indirectly, with the help of the electronic mode such as telephone, radio, cellular phone, voice over internet, etc. It may also be in the form of informal conversation, group discussions, meeting etc.

Oral communication takes place in face-to-face conversations, group discussions, telephone calls and other circumstances in which spoken word is used to express meaning.   *– Ricky W. Griffin.*

It is an effective means of exchange of information because, though the communication is primarily through words, it is carried out with the help of non-verbal cues like body language and voice modulations.

Written Communication

Written communication is a form of Verbal communication. When information, opinions and ideas are exchanged in the written form rather than spoken words, it is known as written communication.

Written communication is, more often than not, formal in nature. This mode of communication, generally used by business organisations, includes letters, reports, proposals, circulars, advertisements, emails, etc. dealt to serve important and multidimensional business purposes. Newspapers, magazines and periodicals etc. too fall under the bracket of written communication.

Non-Verbal Communication

Non-verbal communication is the transmission and reception of meaning between communicators without the use of words, that is, through means other than words. It refers to conveying of emotions, feelings, and messages and flow of information through actions and expressions rather than words. Non-verbal communication takes place through facial expressions, tone of voice, posture, gestures and other body movements and even through space and distance. Simply stated, it is communication other than words. It can include the environment around the communicators, the physical attributes or characteristics of the communicators, and the behavior of the communicators.

Non-verbal communication complements verbal communication. It is an important type of communication in most communication situations, whether informal or formal ones such as interviews and discussions.

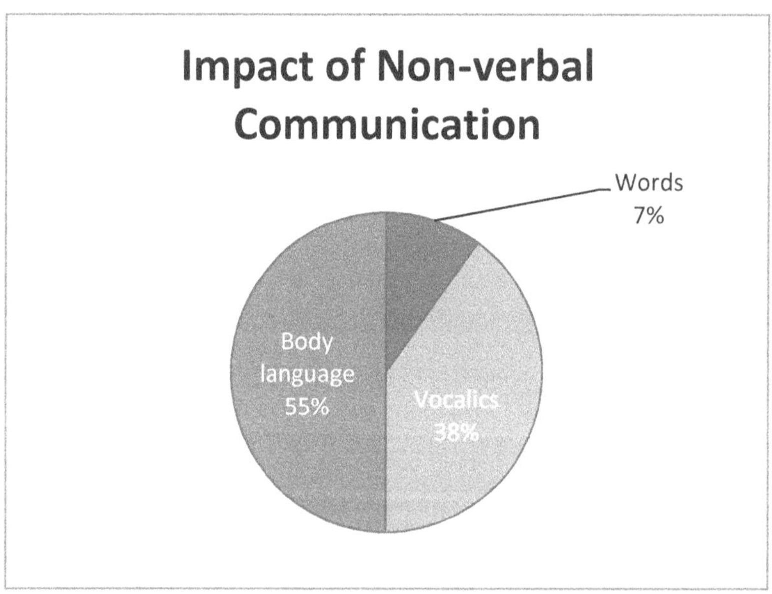

Fig 3: Impact of Non-verbal Communication

Our facial expressions, gestures, body movement, distancing, voice quality and tone, physical appearance, all provide information to the listener/observer and are all significant forms of non-verbal communication. Whereas words are under our conscious control, this is rarely the case with non-verbal behaviour.

Visual, vocal, spatial, and temporal are the four non-verbal communication cues. Each of these relates to one or more forms of non-verbal communication. These forms are:

1) Kinesics: the study of body movement in communication.
2) Oculesics: the study of eye behavior in communication.
3) Proxemics: the study of communication through space and distance.
4) Haptics: the study of communication through the sense of touch.
5) Vocalics or Paralanguage: the study of vocal communication outside of language.
6) Chronemics: the study of communication through time.
7) Olfactics: study of communication through olfactory responses.

Some important non-verbal communication types are:

Kinesics

The word kinesics[2] comes from the Greek *kinesis*, which means 'movement', and refers to the study of physical behaviour in terms of hand, arm, head, eyes, and face movements. *Body Language* is the equivalent popular culture term for it. Kinesics is very important in non-verbal communication, since it can regulate oral communication by substituting words or oral communication entirely, or substantiating the communication by accompanying the words to make them more effective.

Kinesics or Body language stands for the way the body communicates (without the use of words), through posture, gesture, head movements, eye contact, facial expressions, etc., and even silence. Thus, it includes the

---

[2] *Kinesics* as a field of inquiry and research was founded by Ray L. *Birdwhistell*, who coined the term with regard to *body motion communication*. It means 'facial expression, gestures, posture and gait, and visible arm and body movements.

study of the use of bodily movements as non-verbal communication. For example, the blinking of eyes, nodding of the head, shrugging of shoulders, etc. are often used in or as communication.

Kinesics, more formally, is non-verbal behavior related to movement, either of any part of the body or the body as a whole. Every body movement conveys a certain meaning and amounts to non-verbal communication.

Body movements, as mentioned earlier, include gestures, facial expressions and other physical movements. Each of these serves to express or convey information in its own unique way. These physical movements of the body are used and also observed as symbols for communicating non-verbally. These symbols, which are the sources of expression of thoughts, emotions, attitudes and inner body states are largely used subconsciously by the body, though they may also be applied voluntarily.

1) Gesture

A gesture is a body movement intended to convey some specific message. It may be conscious and deliberate or involuntary. Many different intentions, mannerisms, and attitudes can be expressed in gestures. For example, standing up when being introduced to a senior, indicates respect. Gestures may be made with the hands or arms and also include movements of the head, face and eyes, such as nodding, frowning, or rolling one's eyes. Some gestures have an almost universal meaning, such as a handshake universally connotes a "Hello", whereas there are many others that have regional connotations.

2) Facial expression

Facial expressions are a strong medium to convey emotions and feelings. The face can express energy, anger, grief, sincerity and a host of other feelings and emotions[3] which it conveys (mostly involuntarily) as non-verbal communication. For example, a smile conveys friendliness, while a frown means anger.

Facial expressions help in providing information about the communicator, especially, his/her mood, attitude etc. and are very vital in human interactions. Changing facial expressions can change the atmosphere of an entire room and even the direction, perception and impact of a conversation to quite an extent.

3) Posture

Posture is the position adopted by the body, in general as well as in some specific situations. It is an important aspect of body language that has much potential to convey specific meaning. The manner in which one sits, walks or stands communicates much about a person. It conveys a message to the observer, the audience, in every situation that the person is in. The right posture can impress while an uncongenial one (such as slouching, jaw thrusting or arm crossing) can mar a person's impression or image. Posture is nonverbal behavior that can be used to determine a person's degree of attention or involvement.

Posture includes the angle of inclination of a person's body, and the position of the shoulders, back, arms, legs and the head. A raised head indicates openness, kept high both vertically and horizontally indicates confidence and self-assuredness, while a tilted head indicates curiosity or even friendliness. The placement/position of legs too is indicative of a person's body language and is thus also non-verbal communication. It can indicate nervousness, deception, stress etc. Crossing of the legs can indicate disinterest or non-receptiveness and is considered inappropriate during business dealings.

---

[3]Six emotions that are considered universally recognizable are: *happiness, sadness, fear, anger, surprise, and disgust,* and it is observed that almost all cultures use similar basic facial expressions to express these emotions.

4) Appearance and Artifacts

Physical appearance is an imperative part of body language. People are often gauged by their physical appearance, since it makes their first impression in the minds of the viewers. Personal Appearance indicates the degree of importance or interest a person ascribes to an occasion. It is vital for one to look professional and efficient when at work. A shabbily dressed person may fail to make a good impression or even cut a sorry figure before the audience. Clothing, shoes, hairstyle and other accessories and artifacts which an individual dons matter a lot in making his/her first impression as they communicate about him/her before they themselves do. For instance, a good, well-groomed look can indicate a person's good sense of hygiene, good work ethics. It all reflects upon their job, personalities, lifestyles and even values.

Artifacts represent and refer to the various personal adornments such as jewelry, cosmetics, hair adornments and many other objects with which people adorn and surround themselves so as to communicate cultural or personal meanings. These objects profoundly influence communication, since they send out non-verbal cues. People make meaning from these cues based on cultural stereotypes, stipulations, and interpretations.

Emblems

Emblems are non-verbal signals that can be substituted for words and phrases in non-verbal communication. They can generally be translated directly into words since they have a specific meaning understood by all members of a culture. In this regard they are somewhat similar to words, in the context of communication through body language.

Although some emblems can be multicultural, i.e. understood by members of different cultures, most others are either culturally variable or non-universal and call for caution in their gesticulation. The 'thumbs up' emblem for instance, is universal in its meaning of 'liking, approval, or agreement' or even the 'V for victory' gesture which has a conventionalized meaning with a direct verbal translation. On the other hand, the symbol made with the thumb and forefinger, is though multicultural and quick to use, and can be directly translated into its unambiguous meaning "Okay" in most cultures, in other cultures it might be translated as "Zero" or "None".

Emblems have conventionalized meanings and are different from other categories of non-verbal behavior.

Oculesics

Eyes are the most often-used means of communication, both involuntarily and voluntarily. Eye contact is a powerful form of simultaneous communication in any conversation. Through eye-contact the speaker gets signals whether the channel of communication is open/available. Referred to as *Oculesics* in the study of communication, it is a subcategory of kinesics (body language). Oculesics deals with the study of eye movement, eye behaviour, gaze, and eye-related non-verbal communication. Keeping eye contact with the person one is talking to indicates active listening and dedicated attention and helps gauge the other person's interest and response. It plays an extremely important role in communication. Even actions like avoiding eye contact are a form of communication, suggesting 'evasion'.

Why is eye contact imperative in conversation?

1. Eye contact is critical as a way to communicate a vital point across; to show and earn respect.
2. It indicates and affirms that the listener is attentive to, and understands what is being said.
3. Direct eye contact is so powerful that it increases empathy and links together emotional states.
4. Eye contact is critical as it reveals the thoughts and feelings of a person. Humans instinctively establish eye contact to try and understand what a person is thinking.

5. Eye contact projects confidence, self-esteem, and assertiveness while speaking. It helps to establish control (and even dominance) over a communication/situation.

Oculesics is therefore, an essential aspect of effective communication

Proxemics

Proxemics refers to what space and distance communicate to others. That is, the study of space and how people use it when they are communicating, and how comfortable (or uncomfortable) it makes them feel. It is about how we arrange objects and ourselves in relation to space and distance, to include our immediate environment, especially for communication.

Proxemics is defined as "the study of man's transactions as he perceives and uses intimate, personal, social and public space in various settings." – Edward Hall

In terms of non-verbal communication, Proxemics is the study of how humans use space and distance for the purpose. It involves the cues and signals they give to others using personal and social space. These cues and signals can be determined either consciously or subconsciously, depending on how close they perceive a relationship to be. Their setting, such as work or social gathering etc., helps determine these signals and cues. Further, the distances people dictate between themselves and others can vary greatly based on their culture.

The proxemic theory was associated with Edward T. Hall, who first coined the term in 1963. He defined the boundaries and distances which the majority of humans abide by, and described four proxemics space zones[4] starting at 'almost touching', distance between the speaker and the listener.

People tend to unconsciously organize the space around them in concentric zones corresponding to different degrees of intimacy. The size

---

[4]These are also known as *the four types of space language, distinguished depending on distance*, given by Edward T. Hall.

of the zones is determined by a number of factors, such as culture, gender, physical constraints, etc. However, the effect remains the same: that is, the distance/space accounts for the social relation or the level of intimacy between two persons.

The space around us can be defined by four Proxemic Zones (or space languages). These are:

Intimate Space: (within a circle of 1 to 1.5 feet)
The speaker and listener are within a circle of about *18 inches*. One can whisper or embrace in this zone. This space is reserved only for close interactions with people we are intimately close with, such as family members, close friends, and romantic partners. Without both communicating parties agreeing on sharing of this space, it may be considered as an infringement on the space.

Personal Space:(1-1.5 to 4 feet)
The distance between the speaker and the listener ranges from 18 inches to 4 feet, in the personal space. In this circle they comfortably have normal conversations with family members and friends or shake hands with a colleague.

Social Space: (4 to 12 feet)

Here, the scope of the circle extends from 4 feet to about 12 feet. This is the space for interactions with people we don't really know, such as acquaintances or clients at work. This social space language is used for formal purposes. Most business interactions are done within this space, such as addressing a customer or an employee, a presentation at work is a good example.

Public Space: (12 feet to 25)

This zone extends beyond 12 feet (up to25 feet or as far as one can see and hear). In this large space zone, communication becomes formal and distant. Public space is rarely used for interactions apart from public speaking and announcements. An example of this is, delivering a lecture or a speech to a big audience. In it the speaker speaks at a loud pitch so that a large group of the audience can hear him. An infringement on space is unlikely in this space zone.

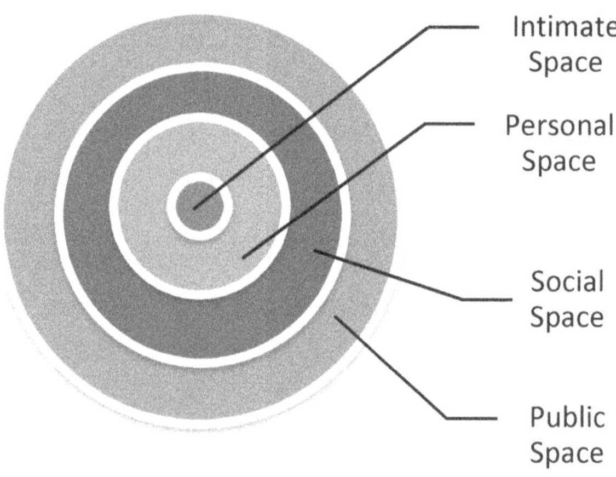

Fig 4: The Four Proxemics Space Zones

Haptics

Haptic communication is non-verbal communication that refers to communication and interaction via tactile contact or the sense of touch. The term 'Haptics' comes from the ancient Greek word *haptikos*. Touch is the most sophisticated and intimate of the five senses. It is crucial in both, human and animal communication since the sense of touch allows one to convey and experience different sensations such as pleasure, pain, heat, cold, etc. Touch can be categorized as positive, playful, control, ritualistic, task-related or unintentional. The sense of touch is the fundamental component of haptic communication for not only interpersonal relationships but also formal communication. A gentle pat on the back; a firm handshake; or even a high five, are some forms of haptic communication, each with its own connotation in the world of communication.

Vocalics or Paralanguage

Vocalics or Paralanguage refers to the non-verbal elements of communication. It is the study of suprasegmental or prosodic features such as tone of voice, in verbal or spoken communication. These are the non-verbal cues of the voice, accompanying speech sounds. That is, they are vocal utterances, *other than words* and serve not just as an additional means/form of communication but an essential one. They can modify meaning or give a nuanced meaning to an utterance, and even convey emotion. Paralanguage may be expressed consciously or unconsciously by the communicator. Vocalics include: pitch, tempo, rhythm, timbre, intonation, stress, pause, intensity, etc. They are somewhat a component of meta-communication[5].

Silence

Silence constitutes an important role in non-verbal communication—as important as speech. It is not merely the absence of any kind of sound. In fact, in communication, it is seen as an absence of speech. The absence of speech doesn't mean that the person is not communicating with the other person. The context of a situation defines the message of the silence. And so, depending on the situation, the meaning of silence differs on each

---

[5] *Meta communication*, referred to as a *communication about communication*, is a secondary communication pertaining to how a piece of information is meant to be interpreted, given that the same message accompanied by different meta-communication can be interpreted to mean something entirely different. *(https://en.wikipedia.org/wiki/Meta-communication)*

occasion. Silence has the potential to lay down the relationship between communicators and their attitude towards each other. Constructive silence can move a conversation or discussion forward as much as words can. It can quite subtly communicate the inability or even unwillingness of a communicator to converse further.

Chronemics

"Chronemics can be defined as the study of human tempo as it is related to human communication." — *Thomas J. Bruneau*

Chronemics[6] is the study of the relationship between time and communication. It refers to the study of how time affects communication and the role it plays in communication. It is one of the subcategories of the study of non-verbal communication. Chronemics is used to understand the use of time in different cultures and helps us to understand how people perceive and structure time in their interaction and relationships with others. The way in which different cultures perceive time can influence their communication to quite an extent. Time perceptions include punctuality, willingness to wait and interact, etc. The use of time by people and cultures affects lifestyles, daily agendas and even how long people are willing to listen.

Given the very concept of communication, the process in itself is a time-bound activity, a person's use of time in the process is an important aspect of communication.

Olfactics

"Olfactics is a form of non-verbal communication where people's reactions are based on smell." —Siegman

---

[6]The term *Chronemics* was coined *by Thomas J. Bruneau,* a professor in communication at Radford University, in the late 1970s to help define the function of time in human interaction.

Olfactics is referred to as the study of olfactory responses as a communicative function. It involves the communicative functions associated with the sense of smell in humans such as body odours, use of perfumes, etc. It is thus, non-verbal communication based on the use of smell or scent as communication. It also involves the perception of different types of scents or odours, which may be genetically or culturally defined. For instance, bad odours are usually perceived negatively, and thus, may result in aversion in communication or interaction. On the other hand, refreshing odours or the use of perfumes indicates an attempt either at communication; establish a favourable impression, or both.

Visual Communication

Visual communication plays an important role in communication. It is communication through the use of visual aid/media; it is the conveying of ideas and information in forms that can be read or looked upon. Visual communication stems from the idea that a visual message accompanying text has a greater power to inform, educate, motivate and/or persuade a person or an audience, because strong visuals can connect with an audience faster, and with more emotion, than words alone and can add new layers of meaning to text. . Visual communication is said to be one of the best means to remove complexity and simplify information in the communication process

Visual communication thus involves visual displays of information like typography, illustration, graphics, photographs, signs, symbols, electronic resources and designs etc. It relies mainly on vision or visual perception.

Communication can also be classified into:

1. One-way Mode of Communication
2. Two-way Mode of Communication

Based on Purpose and Number of Receivers

Different types of communication can be distinguished from the others based on factors such as the number of persons involved, the formality of the interaction, the opportunity to give and receive feedback, etc. For example, communication may be one-way or two-way, or face-to-face interaction.

One-way Mode of Communication

Intrapersonal

Intrapersonal communication is a communicator's internal use of language or thought. It basically takes place in the mind as it is a conversation of a person with self. Intrapersonal communication is commonly known as self-talk since both the sender and the receiver of the communication are the same person. It can be deemed as an attempt by a person to understand and interpret the ideas and thoughts subconsciously passing through his/her mind. A vital aspect of intrapersonal communication involves thinking, analyzing, interpreting, assessing, contemplating, feeling, etc. Although in this type of communication there may be active interaction within the mind of the person, there is no active negotiation of meaning as there would be with another speaker.

Two-way Mode of Communication

Interpersonal

Interpersonal communication is an exchange of information, ideas, and most importantly, meaning between two parties, be they two individuals interacting, or more persons comprising two communicating parties. In interpersonal communication one person's actions both affect, and reflect upon the other's actions. This is because this type of communication often occurs in face-to-face[7] interactions. The term is usually applied to oral communication/interaction that takes place face-to-face, though it can encompass oral, written, and non-verbal forms of communication as well.

In the current scenario, where much communication takes place over media such as the telephone, interpersonal communication doesn't always occur face-to-face. Similarly, in an exchange of text or instant messages, or participating in a chat room communication is between two communicating parties, and is thus interpersonal. It even creates an interpersonal connection of a communicator with another person, but the interaction, though two-way, is not face-to-face. Thus, in interpersonal communication today, the key is an interaction that is done 'in person', that includes at least two participants who bring personal qualities as well as their own thoughts to the interaction, and together, interpret symbols, represent ideas and create meaning, regardless of the medium used.

Group Communication

A group is a number of people with a common goal who interact with one another to accomplish their goals, recognize one another's existence and see themselves as a part of the group. Groups provide an opportunity for people to come together to discuss and exchange views of common interest.

Group communication refers to communication between more than two individuals or communication in a small group. It is an extension of interpersonal communication, where more than two individuals are involved in exchange of ideas, skills and interests. Since this type of communication happens within a small or reasonable sized group, face-to-face communication is possible to some extent in group communication, since it is organised and either only one member addresses the rest of the group or members take turns to address the others.

---

[7] **Face-to-face** interaction allows communicators to communicate both verbally and non-verbally – with words, with gestures, with body language and so on.

Group communication is a mode of communication in an organization, between employers and employees, and employees in teams/groups.

Public Communication

Public communication occurs when an individual or group of individuals sends a specific message to an audience. This is a one-to-many way of communicating. It is exercised when groups become too large to maintain interactions with all group members individually, that is face-to-face.

One of the most common forms of public communication is public speaking. In public communication it is often not possible to receive immediate feedback, unlike interpersonal communication, since the size of the audience is large. The speaker may not have the ability to observe the audience and receive real-time feedback in terms of their nods of agreement or disagreement, or their facial expression, though responses such as clapping may indicate positive feedback.

Mass Communication

"Mass communication is a special kind of social communication involving distinctive characteristics of audience, the communication experience and the communicator." – Charles, R. Wright

Mass communication refers to the dissemination of information from a person, small group of people, or an organization to a large number of (often heterogeneous) geographically dispersed audiences, to accomplish a goal. Through mass communication, information can be transmitted to the audiences quickly, simultaneously and continuously. It requires diverse intermediary channels and communication media to disseminate messages or transmit information to the huge, widely scattered audiences, via mechanisms capable of achieving the task. The major mass media are print (including books, periodicals, magazines, and newspapers), electronic/broadcasting (mainly radio and TV but also other several associated forms such as cable and direct-to-home (DTH) broadcasting) and film (principally commercial motion pictures) etc.

The intent behind mass communication is often to arouse intended meanings in the large audiences in an attempt to inform, influence, entertain or persuade them in a variety of desired ways.

According to R.T. Farrar, "Mass communication is a process by which an individual or organization transmits messages to a large, diverse audience which has a limited opportunity to respond."

Mass communication is a "multi-stage process", opine M.W. Gamble and T.W. Gamble.

Mass communication is distinct from other communication in view of its scale as it essentially addresses a large mass of people.

Based on Organisational Structure

In the organizational setup, there are three *'types'* of communication:

1. Internal and External

2. Formal and Informal

3. Unofficial

Internal and External

Communication in an organisation can be classified mainly as Internal or External, based on the recipient or target audience of the communication.

Internal Communication

Internal communication refers to the way employees interact with one another. It takes place within an office/organization – between employers and employees, among employees, and among different groups/teams of employees. It serves to instruct, inform, direct, educate, motivate, persuade, entertain, develop, caution and control people (and processes) in the organization. Internal communication can be oral or written, visual or audio-visual, formal or informal. It flows in various directions (discussed in the next section).

Some issues that internal communication addresses within an organisation are sharing of corporate concerns, goals, knowledge and skills, performance reviews and appraisals, counselling and training etc.

External Communication

External communication flows outward from an organisation. It refers to the way an organization communicates with the outside world. That is, it addresses people outside the organization, such as prospective or existing clients, business associates, stakeholders, press, media, competitors, public, and the government. It includes Public relations announcements, outreach activities, marketing and branding material/campaigns, job posts, customer service, etc. External communication can take place in various ways and through different channels.

External communication is important for brand building, as well as for maintaining strong customer relationships. All external communication of an organisation should have an overarching tone in order to project a cohesive organisational image. Further, organisations usually have clear guidelines on how to communicate with clients, so as to ensure a consistent, high-quality communication experience for them.

Formal and Informal Communication

Formal communication

Formal communication is a flow of information through formally established channels in an organization. It is the 'Formal' exchange of official information that flows along the different levels of the organizational hierarchy and conforms to the prescribed professional rules, policy, standards, processes and regulations of the organization. Formal communication follows a proper predefined channel of communication and is deliberately controlled. It is governed by the chain of command and complies with all the organizational conventions and rules. This type of communication may be oral or written.

Informal communication

"The informal communication system is built around the social relationship of the members of the organisation" - Herbert Simon

'Informal Communication' is the communication among the people of an organisation based not on formal relationships in the organisational structure but on the basis of informal relations and understanding among employees. It is unstructured and unplanned, and may not be bound by organizational conventions, channels and rules. Informal Communication thus refers to communication on the basis of personal relations that stems from social interaction, and serves to satisfy the natural desire of people to communicate with each other. It employs informal means of circulating information. It is direct, spontaneous, flexible and usually a reliable channel of communication. It supplements formal communication by providing effective feedback to the officials/management. Further, it is helpful in countering monotony and the effects of work-related fatigue. Informal communication is a valuable aid in fostering mutual co-operation and team-building, as also reiterating organizational rules, values and morale.

Informal communication can override formal routes, levels or positions in the organisation, creating a situation where workers communicate with each other, irrespective of their formal positions and relationships. Being informal, it is mostly verbal.

Unofficial Communication

While the ideal communication web in which communication takes place in an organisation, is a formal structure substantiated by the informal channel, unofficial communication channels also exist in organizations. The unofficial channel of communication refers to employee communication outside of the workplace on matters or issues unrelated to or not directly related to work. Social gatherings, friendly meetings and outings among employees are examples of unofficial communication. Office/workplace grapevine too can often be a channel of unofficial communication, though it is at times considered a type of 'informal' communication. The line between the two can be blurred, depending on the nature of the work and the communication. The existence of such channels and flow of information through them brings members to form amiable relationships with each other. They promote mutual understanding and trust and can be beneficial in better work dynamics at the workplace.

Internal and External Communication

Both, internal and external communications are highly important for a business to achieve growth inclusively and function effectively. Internal communication can be used to improve the performance of the organization, by guiding and motivating the individuals to work with higher efficiency. External communication can be used to build a good public image of an organization in the public. An organization aspiring for success should have regular assessment of both the modes of communication.

Internal Communication

Internal communication is a regular aspect of any organization, it occurs when the members of an organization exchange information with each other. This is mainly related to colleagues, co-workers, anyone who is directly a member of the organization or business.

Internal communication is very much important for any firm to grow inside out. It's always preferred that good communication between the members make the firm much standard and stronger from roots. Proper communication can help to solve various problems and adversities.

It is highly used to sort out conflicts and issues of the organization. Well managed and monitored internal communication can help to set a high vision and great goals. Using it effectively will ultimately take the organization to set goals, in time. Good internal communication helps any organization to work smoothly as the lubricant helps a machine to work.

External Communication

External Communication is the transfer of information between an organization and other parties, out of the organization. This mode of communication is basically observed between organizations and clients or customers. The internal members of the organization have the access to this information, but it is majorly for the external members like customers & clients.

It is highly important because ultimately good external communication is advertisements, public meetings, client meetings, Interaction of sales department, social media posts, Newspaper and print media posts, and some online websites or e-stores.

Effective communication helps in upgrading the business, similarly external communication mostly helps the customers or audience to be up to date and grab the latest opportunities available. So, most of today's business world invests a good amount of income to develop external communication and expand the business as much as possible.

Communication will give good profits to any business or organization. Many times, improper information or wrong information may lead to various jeopardized situations. The standard and most successful entities have a highly monitored and well managed external communication system.

External Communication is mostly used for marketing strategies and branding a certain business. Some of the examples of external communication press releases, social media updates, advertising campaigns, email marketing, and website content. The aim is typically to promote sales and publicity, generate sponsorship, announce events, products or services and support branding. Marketing professionals use persuasive techniques to influence others in their external communication strategies.

Based on Direction of Flow

Communication in an organization/office mainly flows in five directions[8]:

1. Downward

2. Upward

3. Lateral or Horizontal

4. Diagonal

5. Outward (External)

---

[8] Aspects of *'Communication Based on Direction of Flow'* have been discussed and substantiated to appropriate detail, as deemed sufficient *in* Chapter 4, *'Communication in Organisations'*. For the sake of avoiding repetition it is briefly touched upon in this section.

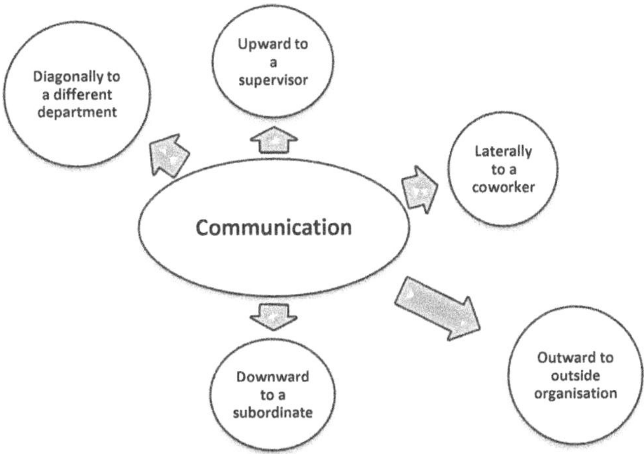

Fig 5: Flow of Communication in an Organisation.

Notes

----

3. Communication Models and Theories

"The most important thing in communication is hearing what isn't being said." - Peter F. Drucker

A model is a systematic representation of an object or event or of real-world phenomenon in idealized and abstract terms. It is a representation which can be applied to different forms. As in all other fields, in communication too models and theories provide important insights into its various perspectives. Different models have been given and interpreted by scholars, to simplify and understand the process of communication. Some of the important models and theories of communication are discussed in this chapter.

Western Communication Theories

According to the western communication theory, the primary goal of communication is to influence through persuasion. The ancient Greek philosopher and scientist Aristotle's 'Rhetoric,' dating back to 4th century BC, is a treatise on the art of persuasion. It is perhaps the first book that deals with the subject of communication. According to his 'Rhetoric', communication comprises three elements — the speaker, the speech and the listener. And the aim of communication is the search of all possible means of persuasion. Aristotle's concept of rhetoric is considered representative of the Western concept of communication, even in the era of mass communication.

Aristotle proposed and wrote about a unique model of communication. He created his linear model of communication placing more emphasis on public speaking than on interpersonal communication. He described three primary aspects of all forms of communication: the speaker, the subject, and the receiver of the message. He argued that it is the listener who ultimately determines the meaning of any particular message.

His model is mainly a speaker centric, where in, the speaker and speech play an important role. The speaker is the active member and the receiver a passive one, in his model. The model indicates that the speaker communicates in such a way that the listeners get influenced, and respond and act congenially. The speaker must therefore, prepare his/her speech and the analysis the audience needs, such that his/her words influence the audience's mind and persuade their thoughts towards his/her communication. His model is primarily a one-way process, which is mainly focussed from speaker to receiver. Even though the model focuses on audience interaction in communication, it incorporates no concept of feedback.

However, Aristotle's model of communication comprises five elements — Speaker; Speech; Occasion; Audience; Effect. The *speaker* must organize his thoughts and ideas and prepare his/her *speech* according to the *occasion* (situation) and target *audience*, in order to obtain the desired *effect*.

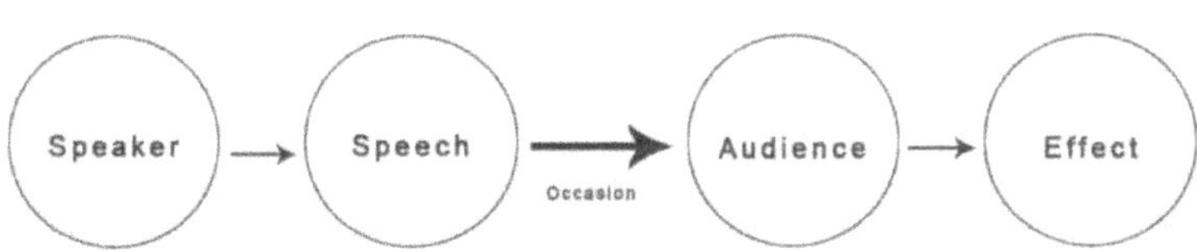

Fig 6: Aristotle's Model of Communication

Aristotle's model of communication is considered as the golden rule to excel in public speaking, seminars, lectures etc. It comprises three components that are considered a must for a speaker to become a good communicator. These are:

1. **Ethos:** In the communication model, Ethos is the characteristic that defines the credibility of the speaker in a communication model.

2. **Pathos:** Pathos in the model helps the speaker to connect with the audience through various emotions like anger, sadness, happiness, confidence, etc.

3. **Logos:** Logos signifies logic. It is an important element of Aristotle's communication model. The audience is influenced by the logic behind the speech.

The Aristotle model of communication is the widely accepted and the most common model of communication, though it has received a fair share of criticism.

Models of Communication

Models of communication make provision of the ways to carry out the processes of communication in a well-organized manner. The field of communication has several models. It is essential to understand how these models work because it helps us make informed choices for our communication.

Types of Models of Communication

The communication process is divided mainly into three standard models that illustrate how communication functions. It is essential to understand how these models work because this informs the choices we make for communication. These models are: linear, interactive, and transactional.

These models are useful because they can help us understand and also identify and explain how different components of the communication process are interconnected.

Linear Model

The most basic model of the communication process, is the Linear model of communication, also known as Straight-line communication. A sender, a message, and a receiver are the three main entities involved in the linear model. The sender encrypts a message and sends it to the recipient via an appropriate channel. The message is decoded by the receiver though there could be obstacles or background noise in the communication process.

The Linear Model emphasizes upon the role of the sender and the message sent. Although the receiver is also part of the communication model, the role of the receiver is quite limited. It is assumed that either the message is received by the receiver successfully or not. In this model, there is no provision to get immediate feedback.

The prominent models of communication that fall under the *Linear* Model are:

1. Aristotle's model of communication
2. Lasswell model of communication
3. Shannon-weaver's communication model
4. Berlo's S-M-C-R model of communication

Interactive Model

The Interactive model of communication is similar to the Linear Model, except that it includes the component of feedback and the aspect of environment (as against merely noise in the Linear Model). Whereas the Linear model of communication views the communication process as 'complete' when the receiver decodes the sender's message, the interactive model does not. As the very name suggests, the communication process in the Interactive Model involves both, the sender and the receiver. It being 'interactive', in this model the sender and receiver are both responsible for encoding and decoding messages. The feedback concept introduced to the Interactive Model gives it a closer simulation of interpersonal human interaction. It is therefore a two-channel model, a fact which imparts it a more dynamic perspective of communication. After receiving the message, the receiver encodes it and transmits a response to acknowledge the message received, to the sender who has now become the receiver.

The Interactive model of communication is more advanced than the linear models of communication. Communication in these models takes place in both directions, and the role of the sender and receiver keeps on inter-changing as the communication proceeds. Communication in the interactive communication models is also known as a *two-way communication* process.

Two models fall under the category. These are:

1. Osgood-Schramm model.
2. Westley and Maclean Model of communication.

Transactional Model

The transactional model of communication is considered to be the most sophisticated model of communication out of all communication models. It is a somewhat more evolved than the interactive model. According to this model, communication is not just an exchange of messages between the sender and receiver. It is a process that creates realities consisting of social, cultural, and relational factors. This model suggests that people don't communicate merely to exchange messages but also to create relationships and to establish communities.

In the Transactional Model, communication is a more dynamic process. The receiver and sender can perform both the roles simultaneously, as messages can be sent back and forth at the same time. People generate common meaning in the transactional model. And for this, the communicators must share at least some degree of cultural, linguistic, or environmental commonality.

There are two models that fall under the category of Transactional Model of communication.

1. Barnlund's transactional model.
2. Dance's helical model of communication.

Ahead, we discuss some of the important models of communication.

Lasswell's Model

Harold Dwight Lasswell, the American political scientist and communication theorist gave an early verbal model in communication in1948.It is a basic but significant communication model and is regarded as one of the earliest and most influential communication models, by many scholars. He posed questions, in answering which one would try to establish the communication process. Lasswell states that a convenient way to describe an act of communication is to answer the following questions:

- *Who*?

- Says *What*?

- In *Which Channel*?

- To *Whom*?

- With *What Effect*?

It is a linear, one-way communication model and gives importance to the communicator and his message. Though it is considered similar to Aristotle's model of communication, it is different in terms of including the concept of effect and also being suited for almost all types of communication. Further, Lasswell offered a broader definition of channel, including mass media along with verbal speech as a part of the communication process. His model suggests that there could be a variety of outcomes or effects of communication such as, to inform, to entertain, to aggravate and to persuade **(Brent, 1984).** His approach also provided a more generalized view of the goal or effect of communication than did the Aristotelian perspective.

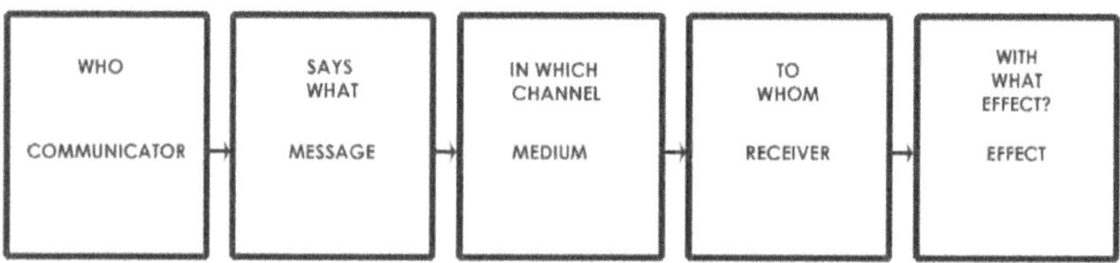

Fig 7: Lasswell Model of Communication

Shannon-weaver's communication model

In 1948, Shannon, an American mathematician, electronic engineer and Weaver, an American scientist joined to write an article in "Bell System Technical Journal" called "A Mathematical Theory of Communication" and also called as "Shannon-Weaver model of communication".

This model is specially designed to develop the effective communication between sender and receiver. Also, they find factors which affect the communication process called "Noise". At first the model was developed to improve the technical communication. Later it's widely applied in the field of Communication.

The model deals with various concepts like Information source, transmitter, Noise, channel, message, receiver, channel, information destination, encode and decode.

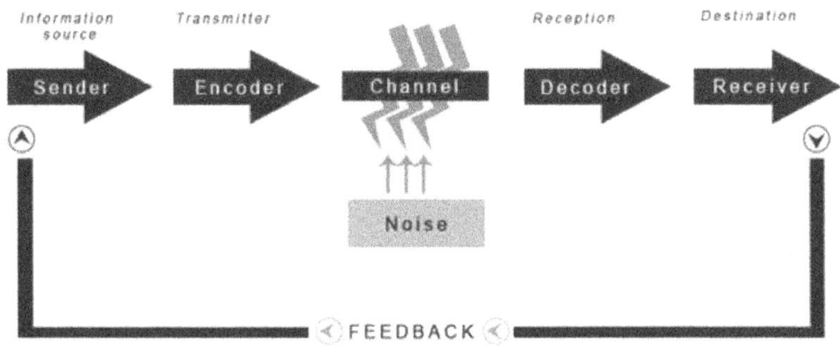

SHANNON-WEAVER'S MODEL OF COMMUNICATION

Berlo's SMCR Model of Communication

In 1960, David Berlo postulated the SMCR model of communication. It represents the process of communication and describes the different components that form the basic process of communication, in its simplest form. Berlo saw communication as a process and the events and relationship of this process as dynamic and on-going.

This model takes into account the different aspects of the message (content, elements, structure, treatment, code). It equalizes both the sender (also called the source) and the receiver. The source is the one from whom the thought originates and who transfers the information to the receiver carefully placing the thoughts and ideas into words. The model gives that ideal communication occurs when both sender and receiver have the common expertise in communication skills, the same attitude, knowledge, social system and culture. These factors play a significant role in the communication process as also in the level of encoding and decoding of the message.

Berlo's model emphasizes the common understanding between the sender and the receiver, which is a significant part of communication. It is in this aspect that it differs from Shannon and Weaver's model mostly. Despite the criticism that Berlo's model leaves no place for feedback, and has no barriers or filters, it has its own preferences. Its most important contribution can be the idea that meanings are in the message users, and not in the message, and therefore communicators must explore them from the perspective of their common knowledge and expertise.

Berlo's model of communication operates on the SMCR model. It describes four components of communication that the acronym 'SMCR' stands for.

- S – **Source** or **Sender**
- M - **Message**
- C - **Channel**
- R - **Receiver**

Berlo's Model has mainly, four components to describe the communication process. Each of the components is affected by many factors. However, the model also focuses on *encoding* and *decoding*, which happen before the sender sends the message and before the receiver receives the message, respectively. It is thus outlined into six stages:

1. The **Source**

2. The **Encoding** of the message

3. The **Message**

4. The **Channel**

5. The **Decoding** of the message

6. The **Receiver**

Since it also focuses on encoding and decoding of the message, Berlo's model can be used for more efficient communication.

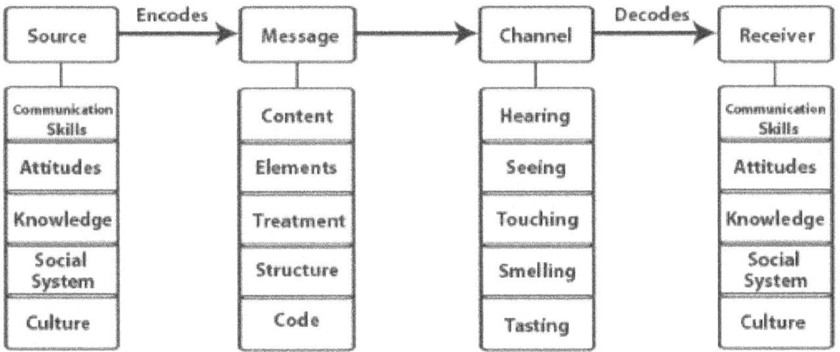

Fig 8: Berlo's SMCR Model of Communication

:

Osgood-Schramm model

In 1954, Charles E. Osgood presented the theory of meaning. Wilbur Schramm changed this theory of meaning into a model and afterwards this model became the Circular Model of communication. The Osgood and Schramm model is about two ways of communication between Sender and Receiver. Osgood popularized the statement that communication is circular rather linear, which requires sender and receiver for sharing their information.

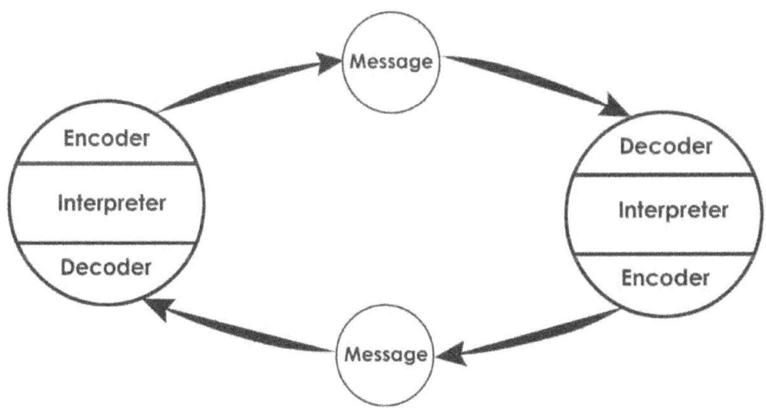

Fig 9: Osgood-Schramm Model

Wilbur Schramm adapted Shannon and Weaver's model of Human communication called a mathematical model but Schramm stressed encoding and decoding aspects as crucial. He defines communication as the sharing of information, ideas, and attitudes.

In Osgood and Schramm model, encoding and decoding is the most important component. In electronic communication, he explains substitute for encoder (microphone) and decoder (earphone). In his model, he considers encoder and source as one person and decoder and destination as another. Here signal is language and you are talking about human communication.

Indian Communication Theories

Bhava

Sadharanikaran

Sahridaya

Sahridayata

The model comprises the following elements:

1. Sahridayas (Preshaka, i.e., sender, and Prapaka, i.e., receiver)

2. Bhava (Moods or emotions)

3. Abhivyanjana (Expression or encoding)

4. Sandesha (Message or information)

5. Sarani (Channel)

6. Rasaswadana (Firstly receiving, decoding and interpreting the message and finally achieving

the rasa)

7. Doshas (Noises)

8. Sandarbha (Context)

9. Pratikriya (Process of feedback)

Indian communication theories are rooted in Indian religious literature, Indian philosophy and fine arts. It was first used in the 10th century commentary called "Natyashastra" by Bharata, the principal source of information for the Indian theory of communication.

The closest word to communication in Indian classical literature is "Sadharanikaran." which translates to 'Universalization' or 'Commonisation'. This Sanskrit term comes closest to the sense of common or commonness usually associated with communication.

The most important assumption in the process of "Sadharanikaran" is that it can only be understood by the 'Sahridayas'. It literally means one heart, or one who has the capacity to receive the message.

Communication according to "Sadharanikaran" is a relationship based on common and mutual understanding and feeling for Sahridaya. This innate ability is acquired through culture, adaptation and learning.

The primary focus in the Indian tradition of communication is an inward search for meaning, a process leading to self-awareness, then to freedom and finally to truth. Thus it transcends language and meaning and is interpretation or reception oriented. The intra-personal communication is of greater importance than inter-personal communication.

The goal of "Sadharanikaran" is not persuasion but the very enjoyment of disseminating and receiving the message. Here the source is perceived as having the higher status, and the relationship is hierarchical of domination and subordination. The source is held in high esteem by the receiver of the information, a relationship that is idealized and romanticized.

Some argue that the asymmetrical aspect of "Sadharanikaran" helped the blooming of Indian civilization in earlier times through efficient communication. However, others argue that it has resulted in a highly rigid and hierarchal closed social structure. The debate continues.

Apart from literature, Indian communication theories are also grounded in fine art traditions. It is composed of permanent mood called "bhava" and illustrated through the dance form. The essence of communication lies in achieving commonness and oneness as stressed in Bharata's Natyashastra.

These moods are capable of arousing corresponding state of feelings. There are nine permanent moods that give rise to nine forms of aesthetic pleasure. For example; 'harsha' joy, 'hasya' laughter, 'irshya,' jealousy, 'karuna', compassion etc

The entire range of human emotions is compressed in this categorization. The nine permanent moods are accompanied by many feelings and are secondary moods that are common to several dominant moods. It serves the purpose of completely manifesting the permanent mood and makes

the communication process complete.

Indian communication theories are also identified through mass communication. It is synonymous with simplification and illustration. Saints and Sufis propagated their message of peace and harmony through simplification and illustration of their messages.

Notes

----

4. Communication in Organisations

"Organisational Communication is the process by which individuals stimulate meaning in the minds of other individuals by means of verbal or nonverbal messages in the context of a formal organization." — *B.N. Jorosi*

Communication has been defined as *a mutual exchange of facts, thoughts and perception, resulting in common understanding of all parties.* It is thus an integral aspect of organisational setup, processes and procedures.

Communication is a required skill at every level of organizational functioning. The effectiveness, with which a person performs in almost any organization, whether commercial, social, or governmental, depends to a large extent upon the ability to communicate effectively. This is because organisations run on interchange of information, ideas, proposals, goals and objectives across the various rungs of their workforce. This interchange is achieved in an office set up, through interactions such as meetings or conversations, presentations and discussions, through telephone calls and messages via electronic media, through memoranda, and through office co-operation (people working together as a team) etc., which are all different forms of communication.

Need for Communication in Organisations

The need for communication in organisations stems from the basic needs of connectivity and information exchange. Communication is needed in all aspects and areas of work in an organisation for it to run smoothly, since the day-to-day operations and processes in workplaces rely mostly on communication of workflow, instructions etc. Further, the ability to communicate effectively is necessary to carry out the thoughts and visions of an organization to the people.

Scope of Communication in Organisations

Scope, in the context of organisational communication, refers effectively to the sphere of operation (or influence) of communication.

Communication in an office encompasses the collation and dissemination of information of all kinds and in all forms, generation and/or collection of data, decision making and implementation, and management of conflict. It serves primarily to facilitate functions such as marketing, accounting, production, sales and so on.

An employee today, must be skilled in communicating effectively, be it within the office (with colleagues across departments, superiors, subordinates) or on its behalf (with clients). This counts as a measure of his/her performance and success at work. It is very important that all organisational communication fits with the organisation's mission, ethics, and industry, since organizational communication provides direction to the organization and its members.

Role of Communication in Organisations

Communication plays a fundamental role in balancing organizational and individual objectives. It provides direction to the organization and its members; guides and motivates them towards the attainment of organizational goals. Organisational communication also provides answers to all questions, clearing up confusion and builds professional relations, thus minimizing conflicts and fostering cooperation.

Used appropriately, communication can be one of the most effective instruments for the growth and development of organisations and their members. Absence of communication on the other hand, or its inappropriate use can engender conflicts and problems.

The role communication plays in an office may be summed up as:

i. Facilitates planning, organising and co-ordination;

ii. Means to establish and maintain cordial relationships;

iii. Facilitates timely and appropriate action;

iv. Aids in decision-making;

v. Helps in problem-solving;

vi. Means of conflict management;

vii. Eliminates the scope for misunderstandings;

viii. Improves motivation and morale.

Importance of Communication in Organisations

Organizational communication is central to organizational success.

Sharing of data and research, explaining plans and policies, imparting training, issuing instructions and orders, counselling, motivating and collecting feedback are all accomplished within organisations by means of communication. It is communication that carries instructions, information, strategies and policies across an organization. Also, communication is essential for building a positive workplace culture, and for conducive teamwork.

The quality of communication in an organisation determines the quality of relationships and also of the environment of the organisation.

The success of an organisation is directly proportional to effective communication in the organisation, as good communication paves the way to achieving effective management. It is very significant for the basic management functions of 'Planning', 'Organizing', 'Directing' and 'Controlling', since all activities in an organization right from assigning workflow rely entirely on communication, especially in today's dynamic work scenarios. Further, communication is the essence of the social system of an organization. It is through communication that relationships between the superiors and the subordinates get established and grow in organisations. The process of communication, thus, is the life force of any organisation.

Advancement in information and communication technologies in today's world has increased the scope of communication in organisations a great deal, irrespective of their scale and type. Communication across offices (global communication) is now facilitated, leading to a spurt in the involvement of employees and the level of their participation in strategic decision making, which is not limited to the local level anymore.

A collaborative environment and open approach to communication in an organisation helps set common goals, expectations, practices, beliefs and value systems and aligns perspectives. Consensus of employees in strategic decision making aligns individual and organisational goals and objectives. Open channels of communication often also lead to an open, transparent organisational culture, since its communication style directly reflects upon its culture which is a natural extension of it.

Objectives of Organisational Communication

The objectives or purposes that are met through communication in organisations are:

1. Conveying information: Knowledge, skills, important messages, information, details and facts about various operations, processes and procedures that are employed in organisations and

technologies they use, are all shared through communication. Thus 'Informative communication' is used in organisations too.

2. Persuasion or influence: The need to influence and persuade others is as relevant in a work scenario as in other areas of human interaction. People must communicate effectively in order to influence, convince or persuade their colleagues, subordinates and superiors, clients, customers, associates etc. within and outside of the work place. This they do through 'Persuasive' communication.

3. Facilitate social interaction: Society has strong expectations about how others should conduct themselves in various social situations. Social norms such as those of greeting and leave-taking, telephone and table etiquette are some expected social behaviours. All these social interactions and most others are as much an integral part of organisational communication as that of personal communication. 'Ritualistic communication' is the process through which people meet all social expectations and carry out social interactions and communication personally or as part of an organisation.

4. Enforcement of rules, regulations norms and discipline: An organisation must convey to its employees, its expectations from them. It must instruct its employees with regard to its mission, vision, rules, norms etc., in order to attain its goals. Inspiring communication helps the employees realise and value its mission statements. It stimulates the employees to abide by the policies and practices of the organization. This ensures better coordination and higher efficiency at work.

5. Express creativity: Creative expression is a human need that prompts 'Imaginative communication'. While day dreams may be a creative expression limited to oneself, inventing and sharing fiction, jokes, poetry, plays and so on, are all ways for humans to communicate thoughts, ideas and imagination to others.

6. Express feelings and emotions: Humans constantly experience the need to express feelings about people, places, objects, events, policies, opinions and ideas, and also, emotions such as joy, sorrow, fear, anger, satisfaction, disappointment etc. These are expressed through appropriate gestures, facial expressions or in words. This form of communication is called 'Affective communication' and plays a vital role in work/office scenario as well.

Factors Affecting Organisational Communication

Group Dynamics

Group dynamics refers to the behavioural and attitudinal characteristics of a group. The system of behaviours and psychological processes occurring within a social group (intragroup) or between social groups (intergroup) is defined as group dynamics. It is concerned with how groups form, their structure and process, and how they function. Group dynamics are relevant to both formal and informal groups of all types, and to intragroup and intergroup behaviours and psychological processes.

The concept of group dynamics is used as a professional tool for problem-solving, teamwork, and to enhance productivity in organizations. Group dynamics can also be used for understanding decision-making behaviour and following the emergence and popularity of new ideas and technologies, in workplaces.

Group Cohesion

Cohesiveness refers to the quality of forming a united whole. In terms of a group, therefore, cohesiveness refers to the bonding of group members and their desire to remain part of the group. It is the degree of closeness among members of a group; the degree to which these members are motivated and attracted by each other. Terms such as solidarity and morale are often used to describe it. Group cohesion is the process that keeps the members of a social group connected. Members of a highly cohesive group are usually seen to develop some common characteristics such as mutual respect, a shared sense of purpose, commitment to the decisions made by the group and accountability to the group. They identify with the collective identity; experience a moral bond to the group; and have a desire to remain part of it. A group usually establishes a structured pattern of communication of its own.

There are many factors that influence the degree of cohesiveness of a group. The more time the members spend together as a group the more cohesive the group becomes. It is for this reason that smaller groups tend to be more cohesive as their members spend considerable time together. Groups also tend to become cohesive within, when faced by intense inter-group competition or a serious external threat to survival. Trust, past group experiences, similarity among members in terms of mindset, values, beliefs, life circumstances, or pressing life issues are some other factors that influence a group's cohesiveness.

Cohesiveness in work groups is considered to be one of the most important and desired characteristics and is often associated with group performance. It has many positive effects, including work satisfaction, low absenteeism, and high productivity. However, highly cohesive groups can be detrimental to organizational performance if their goals misalign with the organizational goals.

Group Formation

Human beings have an innate desire for belonging to a group. Groups, small or large, are seen coming together and working together in organizations as well as in societies. A group can be defined as several individuals who interact with one another, are interdependent, share similar characteristics, and collectively have a sense of unity such that one person's actions have an impact on the others', who come together to achieve particular objectives, accomplish a particular task or goal or for social interaction. A group, more often than not, has certain common objectives & goals because of which members are bound together with certain values, norms and a culture. Group dynamism is bound to occur within a group.

Stages of Group Formation or Development

Bruce Tuckman proposed the four-stage model called 'Tuckman's Stages for a group' in 1965. He however, later added a fifth stage to his model. Tuckman's model states that the ideal group decision-making process should occur in four stages. It explains that as the team develops maturity and ability, relationships establish, and its leadership style changes from being imperative to more collaborative or shared.

Tuckman's 5 stages of group development are:

1) Forming

2) Storming

3) Norming

4) Performing

5) Adjourning

These stages of group formation are meant to be followed in the exact sequence as they are mentioned above.

Forming

This is a beginning stage and lasts only a few days (or weeks). It is the stage of pretending to get along or get on with others in the group. The emotions at this stage are positive. Members begin by planning their work and their new roles. The group begins by learning about team processes.

It is crucial for them at this stage to learn various aspects of communication, conflict resolution, group decision-making and time management, and preparation for the rough times ahead.

Storming

Storming is the second stage of group development. It is a turbulent stage at which the group arrives. It is a stage where the members of a group have understood the work and their sense of competition is at a high level. Therefore, a considerable number of arguments and disputes arise. The group members let down their politeness barriers and try to get down to the issues even though tempers tend to flare up. As the problem of getting along festers the job remains undone. People begin to feel the stress of frustration, resentment, and anger and other such emotions. However, they are normal, natural, and even necessary events in the group development process.

Usually, the storming period lasts 1-2 months. It is critical for the group to handle this stage well as it lays down the foundation to build skills and confidence for the next stage. At times the group requires effective training and support externally since without it the team could experience retarded growth. This is because, if distrust persists, a group may never even get to the norming stage.

Norming

In the norming stage, which is the third stage of group formation, the group works through/beyond individual and social issues. Its members start getting used to each other and developing trust. It establishes its own norms of behaviour and the interaction among the members is eased. Moreover, at this stage, the group develops interpersonal skills, and thus it becomes all the more skilled, productive, and cooperative. Members begin problem-solving. They also cross-train and learn new and adequate job skills. This stage usually lasts for 4-12 months.

Performing

The performing stage begins when the group is comfortable working as a unit and ends when its job is completed. This is the fourth stage of group development. At this stage, the group members have become well acquainted with one another and the group has clarity with regard to what needs to be done. A sense of belongingness is established within the group and it is ready to begin performing its respective task and assigned jobs. Because the talents, skills, and experience of each group member are acknowledged, the morale and the energies to work in a group towards a common goal on a highly efficient and cooperative basis, are high. The work becomes more flexible and efficiencies increase.

Adjourning

Post the performing stage, the fifth stage in group development is reached. The adjourning stage ends the process of group formation. This is the stage for the dissolution or adjourning of a group. It may also be referred to as *mourning*, (that is, the stage of mourning the adjournment of the group). This stage is very crucial in group development since it shows that the task or project that is assigned to the group is completed and has come to an end so the group is to be adjourned.

Need for Group Formation

There are several reasons why individuals join groups. These reasons can vary from need for a self-empowerment to social connectivity etc. The following are some of the needs/reasons for which individuals join groups:

1. Security Needs: Joining a group provides a sense of security and safety to individuals by making them feel that they are not alone. They feel well equipped to deal with external pressures by belonging to a group. For example, workers join trade unions for this sense of safety and security.

2. Social needs: Individuals join groups to satiate their social needs such as the need for belongingness, friendship, social relations.

3. Esteem Needs: All humans have the innate need for growth, recognition, and appreciation for their efforts and achievements. Joining a group, along with a sense of belongingness, provides them with a platform that can cater to this need. When as a member of a group a person does some tasks well and gets recognition and praise from the other members of the group, on the one hand he/she feels a sense of fulfilment of his/her need for growth towards higher achievement at work and for better career prospects, on the other.

4. Power of Unity: As part of a group one most often feels more empowered as compared to standing as an individual, since groups as entities represent power and also offer the same to their members. This helps them to feel secure and protected from undue pressures and unreasonable demands.

5. Identity: Inclusion in a group is important for individuals because it provides status and recognition to them. This meets their need for having an identity in a work or social environment.

Types of Communication in Organisations

Communication carried out in an organisation is mainly of three types:

1. Internal
2. External
3. Unofficial

Internal Communication

Internal communication refers to the way employees interact with one another. It takes place within an office/organization – among employees, among different groups of employees and between employers and employees. It serves to instruct, inform, direct, educate, motivate, persuade, entertain, develop, caution and control people (and processes) in the organization. Internal communication can be oral or written, visual or audio-visual, formal or informal. It flows in various directions (discussed in the next section). Some issues that internal communication addresses within an organisation are sharing of corporate concerns, goals, knowledge and skills, performance reviews and appraisals, counselling and training etc.

External Communication

External communication flows outward from an organisation. It refers to the way an organization communicates with the outside world. That is, it addresses people outside the organization, such as prospective or existing clients, business associates, stakeholders, press, media, competitors, public, and the government. It includes Public relations announcements, outreach activities, marketing and branding material/campaigns, job posts, customer service, etc.

External communication can take place in various ways and through different channels. External communication is important for brand building, as well as for maintaining strong customer relationships. All external communication should have an overarching tone in order to project a cohesive organisational image. Further, organisations usually have clear guidelines on how to communicate with clients, so as to ensure a consistent, high-quality communication experience for them.

Flow of Communication in Organisations

Communication is the life blood of any organisation and must constantly flow in various directions for an organisation to run smoothly. In the process, communication can happen *upward, downward, laterally* and *diagonally* within an office. In addition, official communication also flows outward or externally, to another organisation or office. Thus, communication of an organization/office mainly flows in five directions:

1. Downward
2. Upward
3. Lateral or Horizontal
4. Diagonal
5. Outward (External)

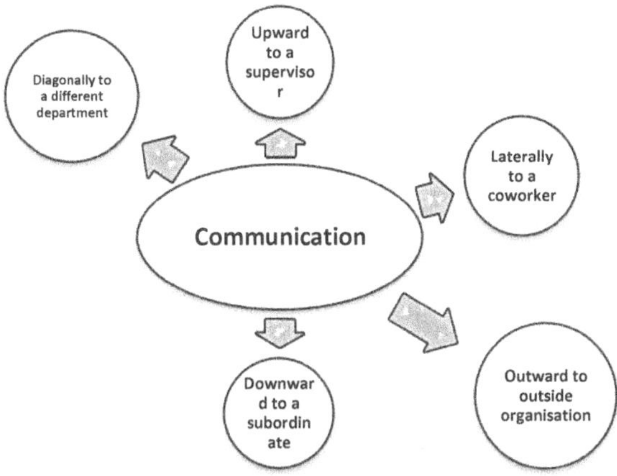

Fig 10: Flow of communication

Downward Communication

Almost all organisations, whether big or small have a hierarchical set up. The flow of information from the higher rung to a lower one, in an organisation is downward communication. That is, the communication from superiors to their subordinates. Downward communication usually includes instructions and information pertaining to the workflow, organisational goals, objectives and expectations. The motto, mission, vision and best practices of the organisation also flow downward in organisations. Notices, circulars, appointment orders, letters and feedback to employees are all examples of *Downward Communication* in an organisation. Communication that flows from regional, zonal or head offices to branch offices is also downward communication.

Upward Communication

Communication that flows from a lower level to a higher level in the hierarchical setup of an organization is categorised as upward communication. In other words, any communication that moves from employees to their supervisors, managers, and so on, is referred to as upward communication. Similarly, communication that flows from branch offices to regional, zonal or head offices is also upward communication. Examples of upward communication include employee suggestions, feedback, complaints, requests, reports, self-appraisal, letters from employees, resignations etc. Upward communication also takes place as a response to downward communication.

Lateral Communication

The communication that takes place in the linear or horizontal direction within an office/organisation is referred to as lateral communication. It takes place at the same hierarchical level, that is, among peers at different rungs of an organisation. It is therefore also called 'Peer-level Communication'. Lateral communication facilitates knowledge and information sharing among peers in an organisation and fosters cooperation and coordination.

Diagonal Communication

Communication that takes place between a supervisor or manager and employees of departments/workgroups that do not (directly) lie on the purview of his/her management, is called diagonal communication.

Outward Communication

Outward communication refers to that communication which takes place between a manager (or some other member) of an office/organisation and external groups such as - suppliers, vendors, banks, financial institutions, media organisations, public relations agencies, etc.

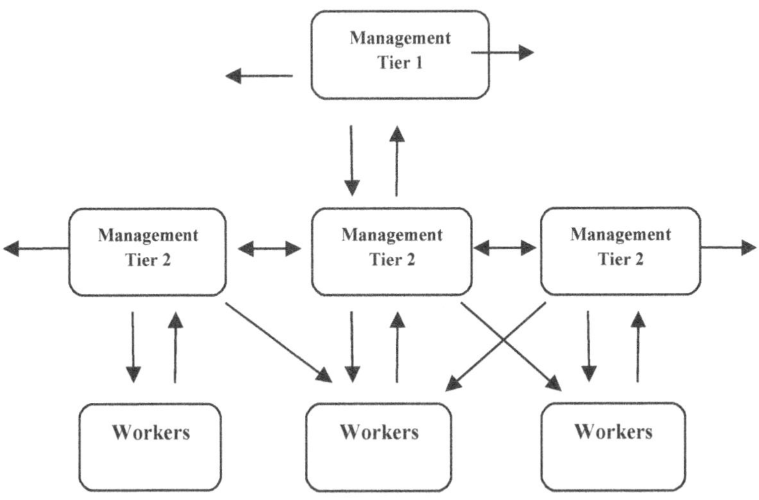

Fig 3: Flow of communication in organisations

Channels of Communication

Communication is vital, to drive innovation and progress in the workplace, as well as for employees to align with the business objectives and goals. This is made possible through proper communication channels. Communication channels are the means by which people in an organisation communicate and interact with one another. Communication flows in an organisation mainly through three channels:

1. Formal
2. Informal
3. Unofficial

Formal Channel of Communication

Formal communication refers to interchange of information officially. It is often characterised by well-defined hierarchical patterns and periodicity. Formal communication is a structured, goal oriented and rational communication; controlled, orderly, effective. It is a deliberate effort ensuring that information is relayed without any hindrance and in a proper and cost-effective way. Formal communication is also known as 'Through Proper Channel Communication'. Messaging/communication in this type of communication channel follows a chain of command. That is, information flows from a manager to his subordinates and they in turn pass on the information to the next rung of employees.

Organizations develop formal, standardised reliable systems of communication for the purpose. Periodical conferences, review meetings and meets are examples of forums that aid formal communication. A formal communication channel transmits information such as the policies, goals and procedures of the organization. Some important means that facilitate the flow of formal communication in an organization are memos, circulars, guidelines, instructions, agreements and reports etc.

Some Types of Formal Official Communication Channels

Telephonic Communication

The telephone has been an indispensable part of human life, be it personal or professional, ever since its induction into the world of communication. It is a source of flow of immense information and allows communication with the outside world.

In spite of the rapid changes in technology over the years, the importance of telephone communication has not diminished. The advantages of actually speaking to a customer or co-worker are many, compared to communicating via text, be it an email or some other type of written messaging. Telephonic communication, being instantaneous, is often more effective and time-saving than written communications such as email and texting. It is mainly for this reason that telephone calls are one of the most common ways a business communicates with its customers.

It saves the customers the time and effort of visiting the company office or sending an email and waiting for a response.

Advantages of Telephonic Communication

1. It is Much More Personal

A phone call is the next best way to connect with a client or business, after face-to-face communication. It is much more personal than an email, text, or social media message and so, the closest one can get to communicating personally. Talking with clients on the phone goes a long way in developing a good relationship and rapport with them.

2. Tone of Voice Comes Through More Clearly on a Telephone

Of the three elements in any face-to-face communication—words, tone of voice, and body language, two, that is 'words' and 'tone of voice' are employable in a telephonic communication. The tone of voice of a speaker plays a very important role in making communication effective, (in the absence of eye contact and kinesic communication) by substantiating the words whereas written communications can use only words to convey a message, which, by themselves, account for a very small percentage of effectiveness for building rapport.

3. Telephonic Communication Facilitates Immediate Response

Communicating a message over a phone call fetches an immediate (initial) response from the person on the other end of the line, thus making communication faster and also, more satisfying since it doesn't involve a waiting time to receive the response, as against written messages.

5. Urgent or Sensitive Issues Better Handled Via Telephonic Communication

Messages regarding urgent, sensitive and confidential issues such as administrative instructions or disciplinary problems are better conveyed via telephonic communication, since they may not be able to allow a wait time. Making calls for such matters conveys to the receiver, their importance and the priority and value ascribed to them.A two-way conversation regarding sensitive topics/issues ensures that the message is rightly interpreted and well understood.

6. Teleconferencing is Cost-Effective and Time-saving

Teleconferencing is an effective option to bring employees of the organization together, remotely, for communications such as meetings. It can be done at a fraction of the cost in terms of time and travelling. These calls can be done using video conferencing over the Internet, if required, in meetings where presentations are to be made.

An organisation sets up an office or an entire department to handle telephonic communications based on the frequency and length of calls required to be made.

A telephone conversation typically includes five stages based on the standard pattern composed by David Taylor and Alyse Terhune:

1. **Opening:** Both parties identify themselves and greetings are reciprocated.

2. **Feedforward:** Purpose and tone of conversation are established. Permission is given to continue (or not)

3. **Business:** Substance of conversation is discussed. The purpose of the telephone call is resolved. The work gets done.

4. **Feedback:** Indicates that business is concluded. Recap of the conversation is done and the next steps are set, if there are any. The talking points are clarified, restated or discussed to arrive at a mutual

understanding. Because telephone conversations lack nonverbal cues, they require additional attention to feedback.

5. Closing: Both parties say thank you and goodbye.

Telephone Etiquette

The objective of any communication is to send a message across to the receiver such that (listener in the context of telephonic communication) it appears just as the sender wants it to be understood. They do not want the listener to understand it otherwise. Given this, it is very important to word the message appropriately and unambiguously to be able to express the ideas accurately such that they cannot be interpreted in different ways. The message should be related to the context and the situation. Since the meaning of an utterance also lies in the non-verbal cues apart from the words used, these play a very vital part in communication. And for this reason, they should form an integral part of telephonic etiquette.

However, most non-verbal cues such as eye contact and kinesics communication (body language) are absent in the case of telephonic communication. The entire onus of communicating effectively lies on the 'words' and the 'tone of voice'. And, since a telephonic conversation lacks the other nonverbal context, it must be ensured that the tone of voice accurately communicates the intended message. The choice of words and how they are said, including spaces or pauses, their pace, rhythm, articulation, and pronunciation are relevant factors in effective delivery of telephonic messages.

Effective skills in telephonic communication go a long way in helping a person make communication successful. Thus, knowing how to use the telephone for official/business purposes (that is having telephone etiquette) is important. It is a means to communicate instantly and effectively, and one needs to manage its use in terms of the manner of communication, along with the information actually being delivered.

In the case of business enterprises/organisations, telephone etiquette /skills are essential to the clients' perception of the organization and their loyalty to it. On the contrary, failure in effective communication due to faulty telephonic communication on the part of a business/organization can bring into question its professionalism and credibility. Here are some points to consider so as to ensure that a telephonic communication is effective:

1. Speaking slowly (at a reasonable pace) and articulating your words clearly.

2. Being specific and to the point.

3. Use of vivid terms and professional terminology to create and sustain interest.

4, Keeping the tone of voice appropriate and professional.

Further, the normal pattern of speech doesn't have to be slowed down by a large degree, but each word should be lent the time and space enough to be clearly discerned and understood by the listener. Else, in the absence of proper junctures (or transitions) the words may seem to run together, losing meaning and creating possibilities for their being misunderstood or misinterpreted.

Repeating any specific information such as an instruction, address or a phone number etc., (or asking to repeat for confirmation) as necessary, is good etiquette in telephonic conversation.

Like most other communication, telephonic communication too is a two-way process. And feedback, the response from the listener to the speaker, is also an essential element of phone conversations. Thus, good telephone etiquette is important while making as well as while receiving calls, in order for the calls to be managed professionally.

Informal Channel of Communication

Informal communication is a vital element of communication in any office. It is the casual and unofficial form of communication wherein the information is exchanged spontaneously. It takes place in an unstructured manner and outside the formal systems and forums without having to conform to the prescribed official processes, rules, formalities and chains of command. Informal communication is used more often in situations where there are no rigid hierarchical tiers. This form of communication takes place through informal talks, conversations and chats etc., that have no set direction. They evolve from interpersonal and social interactions among employees.

> "The informal communication system is built around the social relationship of the members of the organisation." - *Herbert Simon*

Grapevine

In the organizational framework, informal communication is also termed as grapevine or grapevine communication. This is because it travels through indefinite channels of communication and it is difficult to define the beginning and the end of the communication. There is not any definite chain of command[9] through which the information flows. Therefore, in informal communication systems, information can flow from anywhere. Rumour and gossip also fall under the purview of informal communication.

Unofficial Channel of Communication

Communication in organisations is not limited to being official only. There is an unofficial channel of communication too. It refers to employee communication outside of the workplace or workplace matters/issues, on

---

[9] *'Chain of command' refers to a line of authority where authority flows from top to bottom in an organizational structure.*

matters unrelated to work. Examples of an unofficial communication channel include social gatherings, Friendly meetings, dinner outings, among employees. The existence of such a channel and information flowing through it, is but natural.

Along with being classified as Formal, Informal and Unofficial, channels of communication can also be classified based on the manner/method of communication, in business organizations. These are:

1. Digital Communication Channels
2. Face-to-face Communication Channels
3. Written Communication Channels

Digital Communication Channels

Technology has made sure that organisations reach and engage their employees using digital communication platforms. These include a variety of software and tools that employees use in order to stay up to date on official instructions, directions, developments and news and to stay in touch with one another, especially with regard to their (team) work responsibilities. Digital communication channels are thought to be the most effective. A few examples of these are the intranet, employee collaboration software, project management tools, feedback software, social media, etc.

Face-to-face Communication Channels

In spite of the fact that digital and electronic forms of communication seem to be gaining over, face-to-face communication is still vitally crucial in the workplace. It is still the best way to connect with a client or business since it substantiates the spoken word and many situations require this.

Written Communication Channels

Written communication has a niche of its own in terms of business/organisational communication. This sort of communication is quite prevalent and still required when communicating critical policies, via letters, memos, manuals, notices, and announcements to employees. Similarly, for the purpose of external communications with the customers, retailers, distributors and other individuals, the written channel of communication is still the most effective. Emails, live chat, text messages, blogs, newsletters, written documents, etc., are a few examples of communication via this channel.

Notes

6. Technology in Communication

The most technologically efficient machine that man has ever invented is the book.- Northrop Frye

The role that technology plays in the field of communication, in the current times, is no secret at all. Technological changes have been instrumental in changing the way in which communication is carried out in the world scenario, be it personal communication or organisational. These fast-paced enhancements in communication technology have ensured that there is only one direction for it to head to, and that is, forward.

Human behaviour is dominated by communication to such an extent that humans have applied advanced science and technology to the tremendous development of communication systems. With the help of inventions such as printing press, telephone, fax, radio, television, satellites, and many other devices and technologies, they have made communication instantaneous and effective.

Communication in Organisations nowadays by and large operates through (information) technologies, that update quite frequently in the current state of affairs.

New Information Technologies

The growth of telecommunication and information technology has eased the process of communication, be it at personal level or at the level of communication in organisations. The modern world has come a long way from communicating through letters, telegrams and telegraphic messages. These 'traditional' methods or means of communication came to be replaced by faster paced email, telephone, fax and so on. However, the scenario has taken several turns since. People of all age groups now rely mostly on the internet for communication and for information, since this can be achieved by flicking or swiping a finger. A message snippet on a 'Chat Application' goes a long way in this fast-paced world, having easily overtaken most other means of communication. Further, Artificial Intelligence is taking over the world scenario in all fields with chat-bots and speech-based communication becoming all pervasive. Electronic devices can communicate with each other. All such communication is facilitated by the shared understanding of certain symbols and their systematic exchange between the participants involved in the communication process. With newer and newer information technologies coming up, constant changes in the communication scenario shall continue to be the order of the day.

Influence of Technology on Communication

Technology has perpetually paved the path smooth for people and organisations to communicate with one another, by introducing newer channels of communication and improving the existing ones. Web-based evolution in communication technology has revolutionised how people interact in their day to day lives. Newer channels such as online talks, webinars, vlogs and blogs etc. are seen readily dispersing knowledge and information.

Further, introduction of smart technology is a radical change in the way the world communicates. It has, by itself, altered how routine functions are performed. Now, more than ever, people keep up with the pace of technology upgrades. Communication today, is not limited to 'human-to-human' communication with the use of gadgets and devices. Humans now communicate with smart gadgets, getting their tasks done and organising their day-to-day affairs.

Innovative advancements in the field of communication have led to the evolution of a digital platform for communication, through which people can share their skills and ideas. The all-pervasive new technologies have opened the doors of innovative methods to the field of media as well. Online access and sharing of news and information on social media platforms has been made possible only because of the web-based evolution in communication

Influence on Workplace Communication

Communication in Organisations nowadays by and large operates through (information) technologies that update quite frequently. This has played a major part in altering the way in which routine organisational operations and communication are carried out in the current state of affairs.

Technological evolution has changed the channels of sharing and access of information a great deal. Organisations gain better business by connecting with their customers through these channels. This changing scenario has been instrumental in changing how businesses interact with their clients/customers and vice versa. Technological changes have ensured an end to the times when one had to wait for days to receive a response or resolution pertaining to a query. Today, businesses operate on short 'turn-around-times' in attending to the needs of their clients. New web-based platforms enable businesses and their clients to access relevant information and respond to queries, as and when they arise. Organisations leave no stone unturned to serve their customers above and beyond the industry standards and the vast dispersion of technology facilitates this at every step.

The World Wide Web (www) has shrunk the world of business as much as any other aspect of it. Organisations no longer operate from within the four walls of their establishments neither is the scope of their operations limited to local boundaries. These are the times of globalised organisations, given that resources are as handy as being right at the fingertip and information can be had with the mere click of a finger. Having a web presence is the order of the day for any organisation/business, such is the influence of technology. Organisations are proactive in their communication what with resolving their clients' queries through pre-anticipated FAQs (frequently asked questions) and chatbots ready with instantaneous information. Such automated business processes are obliterating the wait time that customers had to endure in the past to get a problem resolved. Thus, enhanced modes of communication relay information in a resourceful manner enhancing the customers' 'user experience'.

Digital communication

Information shared through the screen of a digital device can be called 'Digital Communication'. The term 'digital' refers to any data that is encoded in a machine-readable format. That is, it is represented by a series of digits (1 and 0). Digital communication involves an organization's dispersal of information such as text, audio, video and graphics through an online channel. In their communication efforts most organizations use a wide range of online channels—their websites, chat applications, blogs etc.—to connect and communicate with current and potential customers. This sharing of information over the internet, using electronic devices and innovative channels is digital communication. The widespread use of digital connectivity by organisations has not only reduced their dependence on conventional modes of communication, but also enhanced their business prospects through better and faster connectivity and transparency. They now deliver value-added content to clients easily through digital media.

Further, evolution of social media has been one of the most marked changes in the field of communication. Today, organisations can connect with their customers on these platforms and relay information readily, which might be impossible to do through traditional or 'old world' modes of communication. This ability of users to maintain connectivity on social media platforms continually and to access media such as newspapers, magazines, book etc., in digital form (online) has added much value to the means of communication. Similarly, emails and instant messages have digitalised the day-to-day communication needs of people the world over.

The ability of businesses to readily provide information to their clients digitally through their websites and social media has eased out the task of maintaining public relations a great deal.

Notes

7. Communication and Culture

"Culture is the pattern of taken-for-granted assumptions about how a given collection of people should think, act, and feel as they go about their daily affairs."   *- Joynt & Warner*

The term 'culture' refers to the collective system of sharing and transfer of social behaviour that gives a common identity to a particular group of people at a specific point in time. It is the sum total of the knowledge, language, meanings, habits, hierarchies, history, folklore, customs, rituals, traditions, norms, rules, values, attitudes and so on, cultivated and acquired by a group of people over the course of time and transmitted from generation to generation. Culture influences everything that people do, including the way they communicate. It plays an important role in shaping and defining the communicative behaviour of people. It refers to their manner of communication that is, how they interact socially. Communicative behaviour stems from their cultural affiliations and is greatly influenced by the culture of the communicator.

Communication, on the other hand, being the means of human interaction is a social need of human beings. They interact in individual relationships, groups, and societies, and this social interaction (or *communication*, as it may be called) sets out behavioural patterns. They imbibe these behaviours and habits, the perceptions of the world and morality through interactions in the community and environment they belong with. These perceptions influence what they believe and value, and what rules they live by, amounting to the creation of norms, rules, laws, customs, roles, rituals, etc. (that is, 'culture'). Thus, it is through communication that all social units develop a culture which is essentially a process that encapsulates all societal behaviour.

"Culture is communication, communication is culture."

- Edward T. Hall

The development of human culture is made possible through communication, and it is through communication that culture is transmitted from one generation to another. All activities that transfer meaning, whether through the spoken word or the non-verbal modes amount to communication. In transferring meaning, communicators draw essentially, from factors such as their perceptions, cultural affiliations previous experiences, and the present communication environment.

Culture on the other hand tells people how to respond in a social context. It plays an important role in shaping the manner of communication of people — the way they talk and behave. Therefore, people's communication is guided to a great extent by the knowledge they have about a culture and its influence. Additionally, within every culture there exist sub-cultures that further define and determine the communication its people have. Thus, in order to interpret communication, the culture in which it takes place has to be taken into consideration.

Communication and culture thus, greatly influence each other. In other words, culture and communication are intertwined and are considered to be inseparable.

Organizational Culture

Organizations too have cultures—their own unique cultures, which often reflect in sets of shared assumptions, norms and meanings, principles, codes of behaviour, practices and procedures, dress codes, workspace layouts, leadership styles, meeting styles and manner of functioning, and so on.

The founders' vision and mission of the organisation reflect their beliefs and values and define, design and lead to the formation of their organizations' early cultures, which take shape and gain roots over time. Organizational culture thus, is apparent in the vision and mission statements of the organization and articulates them appropriately. It is reflected in all aspects of the functioning of the organization.

An organization's culture is responsible for creating the kind of environment in which its affairs are managed. It affects how and to what extent employees identify with the organization. It plays an important role in shaping communicative behaviour in the organisation, and even refers to their manner of communication. That is, it affects the way employees interact with one another, with stakeholders, and with clients and so on. Organizational culture defines an organization's effectiveness, for it binds and holds the members of the organization together, inculcating and enhancing teamwork and promoting collaborations. Further, a healthy organizational culture reduces stress, raises morale and job satisfaction, leading to exhibiting uniform conduct and higher performances.

Organizational values are transmitted to new employees through orientation, training, counselling, and mentoring programmes that outline and reinforce the organization's goals or mission statement, core values, and also through participation in the organization's events, interaction with seniors etc. The newcomers of an organization are thus initiated into its culture and they learn to grow and thrive in that culture and embody its value system. The culture thereby grows and prevails throughout the organization.

Communication plays a very vital role not only in delineating organizational culture clearly and consistently to employees but also in its rooting, surviving and thriving in the organization. Thus, organisational communication and culture are mutually dependent, as is the case in all other walks of human life.

Notes

References

Backstrom, L.; Huttenlocher, D.; Kleinberg, J.; Lan, X. (2006). "Group formation in large social networks". *Proceedings of the 12th ACM SIGKDD international conference on Knowledge discovery and data mining - KDD '06.* p. 44

Communication for Business. India, Pearson Education, 1991.

Decoding Communication: A Complete Handbook for Effective Communication. India, Notion Press Media Pvt. Limited, 2021.

Denis Mac quail- Towards a Sociology of Communication – London, collier Macmillan 1975.

Duck, Steve, and McMahan, David   T,.. The   Basics   of Communication: A Relational Perspective. India, SAGE Publications, 2009.

Fielding, Michael. Effective   Communication   in Organisations. South Africa, Juta Academic, 2006.

Fiske, John (1990). Introduction to Communication Studies. Routledge, London.

Hargie, Owen. Skilled Interpersonal Communication: Research, Theory and Practice. N.p., Taylor & Francis, 2003.

Intrapersonal Communication: Different Voices, Different Minds. United Kingdom, Taylor & Francis, 2012.

Jamieson, G. H. Visual Communication: More Than Meets the Eye. Bristol: Intellect Books, 2007. ISBN 978-1-84150-141-3.

REFERENCES

Kenneth Louis Smith (2005). Handbook of visual communication: theory, methods, and media. Routledge. p. 12. ISBN 978-0-8058-4178-7

Lehman, Carol M., et al. Business Communication. United Kingdom, Cengage Learning/South-Western, 2011.

Nonverbal Communication: Science and Applications. India, SAGE Publications, 2013.

Papa, Michael J., et al. Organizational Communication: Perspectives and Trends. India, SAGE Publications, 2008.

Reicher, S. D. (1982). "The determination of collective behaviour." Pp. 41–83 in H. Tajfel (ed.), *Social identity and intergroup relations*. Cambridge: Cambridge University Press.

Rothwell, J. Dan (2010). In the company of others: an introduction to communication (3rd ed.). New York: Oxford University Press. ISBN 978-0-19-533630-6.

Steinberg, Sheila. An introduction to communication studies. South Africa, Juta, 2007.

Sunil Sondhi. Sabdapurvayoga: Indian Communication Theory and Practice. Kalakalpa IGNCA Journal for Arts, 2022.

The Handbook of Communication and Corporate Social Responsibility. Germany, Wiley, 2011.

Theories and Models of Communication. Germany, De Gruyter, 2013.

Verma, Shalini. Business Communication: Essential Strategies for 21st Century Managers, 2e. India, Vikas Publishing House, 2014.